DATE DUE

JUL 19 1996			
WITHDRAWN			

SCRIPTURE PLAYS

SCRIPTURE PLAYS

Ten Plays from the Holy Bible

By
DAN NEIDERMYER

MERIWETHER PUBLISHING LTD.
COLORADO SPRINGS, COLORADO

Meriwether Publishing Ltd., Publisher
P.O. Box 7710
Colorado Springs, CO 80933

Editor: Arthur Zapel
Typesetting: Sharon Garlock
Cover design: Michelle Z. Gallardo

Library of Congress Cataloging-in-Publication Data

Neidermyer, Dan, 1947-
    Scripture plays : ten plays from the Holy Bible / by Dan
Neidermyer.
        p.   cm.
    ISBN 0-916260-57-7
    1. Bible plays, American.   I. Title.
PS3564.E28S37   1989
    812'.54 -- dc19

                                              88-37687
                                                  CIP

To
HILDA SULLIVAN
whose hope and exuberant love of life, have
— like many characters found within the Scriptures —
challenged and inspired not only me, but also
thousands of others in her audiences

TABLE OF CONTENTS

INTRODUCTION

Almost from the beginning of time, drama has been utilized to explain the mysteries of life, earthly and divine.

The Greeks, wishing to describe to its population the reason for the changing of the seasons, brought its citizens to an outdoor amphitheater and showed a chorus interacting with a thespian depicting the mythological explanations for summer, winter, spring, and fall.

Clergy in the middle ages, facing largely illiterate congregations, staged huge "passion plays" dramatizing the events during the last week of Christ's life in an attempt to show the sacrifice of God the Father through his Son, Jesus Christ, for their eternal salvation.

Throughout the countryside, medieval bards and wandering minstrels and troubadours sang of biblical personalities and repeated from village to village the exciting accounts of bravery, courage, love, and sacrifice found within the Holy Scriptures.

Costumed actors stood atop hay wagons pulled into the middle of medieval town squares and dramatized the wisdom of Solomon, the treachery of Ahab, the leadership of

Moses, the eloquence of the psalmist shepherd-king David, and most often, the miracles, parables, and teachings of Jesus.

Most recently, radio, television, and film productions with major international celebrity casts have dramatized much of Holy Writ, bringing to hundreds of millions the excitement, the beauty, the truth that is the Word of God.

Thus, while a student at Philadelphia College of Bible and Temple University, I searched for scripts detailing biblical accounts and personalities that could be easily produced and staged by actors of varied, even limited theatrical experience and expertise.

Finding very little scriptural drama that was suitable, I began to write my own. I wanted to use it to stage the Scriptures in Sunday schools, during worship and junior worship experiences, as part of vacation church school programs, at youth meetings, and children's rallies, throughout Christian education conferences and conventions, in convalescent and nursing homes, and as a means of sharing the Gospel during chapel worship in prisons, hospitals, military bases, juvenile detention centers, mental retardation facilities and for home Bible studies. I wanted biblical drama for use anywhere that Christian people may choose to gather to see actors perform in the service of our Lord.

These dramatizations of biblical accounts were then produced by national and international traveling drama teams associated with the work and ministry of Maranatha Productions, Inc., a nonprofit evangelical ministry and production company.

Drama teams, consisting of from two to five actors, have presented each of these dramatizations hundreds of times. They have been performed in all sizes, types, and kinds of staging situations throughout the United States, the Caribbean, Canada, and Scandinavia. Other drama teams representing organizations, ministries, and producing companies of other countries and other languages have also produced and staged these same biblical dramatizations in a wide variety of places.

These dramatizations have been stage-tested for performance in almost any type of situation utilizing no stage sets, minimal set pieces and props, and with much imaginative and creative blocking.

Casts for each dramatization are small and do not

require actors with great dramatic experience. Any church, youth group, school thespian society, traveling drama team, or producing agency should have no fear about presenting these tested dramatizations.

Casts can easily be expanded if additional actors are available. Also, many roles within these plays can be either male or female characters at the director's discretion and the availability of cast members.

These dramatizations can also be enhanced with music, either vocal or instrumental, appropriate to the time period of the account. In several of these dramatizations, special effects can be used to enhance the theatricality of the presentation. Choices depend on the discretion of the director and upon the technical expertise of the producing group.

Four plays include optional "audience participation". To involve the audience spontaneously and easily within the re-telling of the biblical story often adds considerably to the production.

Drama teams associated with Maranatha Productions, Inc., have found their audiences more appreciative of the message of the play when the scriptural account of the particular dramatization is read before the dramatization and briefly explained.

The Holy Scriptures as the Word of God contain fascinating and exciting accounts of individuals, personalities, and peoples. The lessons and messages, though ancient, are still contemporaneous with modern people. Dramatizing these accounts provides an opportunity to relive these exciting lives and fascinating events of Holy Writ while simultaneously inspiring, edifying, and blessing an audience.

May you enjoy reading and staging these plays. The world is very much in need of hearing and seeing the good news of the Scriptures. That the stage and the dramatic form allows us to bring God's Word to life is a unique thrill that we want to share with you.

Respectfully,
Dan Neidermyer
Executive Producer
Maranatha Productions, Inc.

Section I

PERSONALITIES
of the
OLD TESTAMENT

MOSES
(Exodus 1-12)

Born during the harsh Egyptian edict that demanded the deaths of all male Hebrew slave infants, Moses was placed by his mother in a tiny ark among long-stemmed reeds in the Nile. He was found and later adopted by Pharaoh's daughter. The boy-child was destined to become the greatest and best-known leader of the Hebrew people.

Known as the "Law-Giver," because it was to him the Lord God Jehovah gave the Ten Commandments, Moses lived his boyhood within the Egyptian Pharaoh's palace. But his favored life of luxury and ease abruptly ended one day during an official inspection tour of the difficult working conditions of the Hebrew slaves. There he observed an Egyptian overseer harshly beating a Hebrew slave. Angered by the overseer's severe treatment of the slave, Moses killed the Egyptian and hid the dead man's body within the hot sand of Egypt.

Days later, found out, the Pharaoh demanded his death in retribution. Moses escaped to the deserts of Midian where he found refuge with a priest. He settled there and later was married to one of the priest's daughters. He became a shepherd . . . even as the harsh slavery of his people continued.

The Lord God Jehovah, hearing the cries of his people, appeared to Moses while he tended his father-in-law's flocks. From out of a bush that was on fire but was not consumed by that fire, the Lord God Jehovah commanded Moses to "lead my people, the Israelites, out of Egypt!"

Moses was commissioned in this way by the Lord God Jehovah to confront the Egyptian Pharaoh (historically Ramses II). He was to demand the release of the Hebrew slaves and lead them out of their years of slavery in Egypt to a new land, a "promised land flowing with milk and honey!"

Cast of Characters

MOSES
The Law-Giver
AARON
Brother to Moses
PHARAOH
The ruler of Egypt
MAGICIAN
Adviser to the Pharaoh
GERAH
Adviser to the Pharaoh
THOTMES
The Pharaoh's young son

Note: Though traditionally advisers to the Pharaohs were male, the "Magician" and "Gerah" characters can be either male or female.

Scriptural background for this dramatization: *Exodus 1-12*.

Length of this dramatization: Approximately 35 minutes.

SCENE 1

AT RISE: The MAGICIAN enters the staging area carrying a papyrus scroll. Walking to the front of the staging area, the MAGICIAN unrolls the scroll and begins reading the following narrative *(Exodus 1:8-11; Exodus 3:1-6).*

MAGICIAN: **Then, eventually, a new king came to the throne of Egypt who felt no obligation to the descendants of Joseph.**

He told his people, "These Israelites are becoming dangerous to us because there are so many of them. Let's figure out a way to put an end to this. If we don't, and war breaks out, they will join our enemies and fight against us and escape out of the country."

So the Egyptians made slaves of them and put brutal taskmasters over them to wear them down while building the store-cities Pithom and Ramses.

One day as Moses was tending the flock of his father-in-law, Jethro, suddenly the Angel of Jehovah appeared to him as a flame of fire in a bush. When Moses saw that the bush was on fire and that it didn't burn up, he went over to investigate. Then God called out to him.

"Moses! Moses!"

"Who is it?" Moses asked.

"Don't come any closer," God told him. "Take off your shoes, for you are standing on holy ground. I am the God of your fathers — the God of Abraham, Isaac, and Jacob." *(The MAGICIAN exits.)*

SCENE 2

AT RISE: MOSES enters the staging area, quickly followed by his brother, AARON, who by the intensity and volume of his voice is either protesting or disagreeing with MOSES' statements.

AARON: **But who will believe you, Moses?**

MOSES: **The people of Israel.**

AARON: Why?

MOSES: Why what?

AARON: Why will they believe you?

MOSES: Because the Lord God Jehovah sent me.

AARON: Have you lost your mind, Moses?

MOSES: No.

AARON: Have you gone mad?

MOSES: No.

AARON: But the people of Israel . . . they're all slaves in Egypt —

MOSES: And they're suffering —

AARON: Terribly.

MOSES: All the more reason I must go to Egypt, rally the children of Israel together, and demand of the Pharaoh that he let my people go!

AARON: But the people of Israel will say, "Jehovah never appeared to you, Moses!"

MOSES: But he did.

AARON: Where? When? No man has ever seen God.

MOSES: I don't know that I myself have even "seen" God.

AARON: I knew it.

MOSES: But I have "heard" him.

AARON: *(Exasperated)* Moses!

MOSES: God spoke to me from the flames of a magnificent burning bush.

AARON: *("Sure he did!" kind of attitude.)* A burning bush!

MOSES: That was not, that was never consumed.

AARON: Never consumed!?

MOSES: The flames sparkled brilliantly as they leaped heavenward . . . a continuous fiery brightness . . . more than a burning . . . actually, an ever-increasing, ever-changing shining!

AARON: Moses, even I am having difficulty believing you — talking with God while tending sheep, seeing a burning bush that was never consumed, proclaiming and not contending the Lord God Jehovah challenged you to deliver and lead our people out of Egypt and the Pharaoh's mighty hand!

MOSES: *(Momentarily downcast)* Even you, my own brother, don't believe me.

AARON: And there is something more to think about, Moses! The children of Israel, even as they quarry stone and make the bricks for Pharaoh's pyramids, even as they fall under the harsh sting of the Pharaoh's overseers' whips, these people, our people, will scream out that they have been slaves so long in Egypt — more than four-hundred years — the Lord God Jehovah has surely forgotten them in their bondage and suffering.

MOSES: But he has not!

AARON: Prove it!

MOSES: The Lord God Jehovah appeared to me —

AARON: You're only a shepherd, Moses. The Lord God Jehovah doesn't appear to shepherds, ordinary people!

MOSES: The Lord God Jehovah appears to whomever he wishes.

AARON: *(Agreeing)* Yes, Moses. *(Even more exasperated.)* And what did he say?

MOSES: God said from out of the burning bush: "I have seen the deep sorrows of my people in Egypt and have heard their pleas for freedom from their harsh taskmasters. I have come to deliver them from the Egyptians and to take them out of Egypt into a good land, a large land, a land flowing with milk and honey."

AARON: Even if I did believe you, Moses —

MOSES: You must.

AARON: I must!?

MOSES: You are going to Egypt, also.

AARON: Me? What can I do in Egypt? What can I do against the might of the Pharaoh?

MOSES: You are saying what I myself said . . . at first. So, now you know how I felt.

AARON: *(Momentarily capitulating)* But can you do it, Moses? Can you lead the people of Israel out of their slavery and bondage?

MOSES: At first I shouted to God, "I'm not the person to do this, Lord." But he told me I was creating excuses, that he would give me signs of his power which would become proof to his people.

AARON: Signs? What signs?

MOSES: At his urging, I cast my shepherd's rod, my wooden crook, to the ground . . . and —

AARON: And?

MOSES: That wooden crook became a serpent!

AARON: Your rod became alive?

MOSES: Before my very own eyes even as I watched!

AARON: Amazing!

MOSES: Not when you realize the great power of the Lord God Jehovah, the same God who created the world and the universe, which is ever expanding . . . is making a shepherd's crook writhe as a snake an impossibility?

AARON: Not an impossibility, no, but certainly something no man is able to do.

MOSES: Then I pleaded with the Lord God Jehovah, protesting that I was not a speaker!

AARON: And what was God's answer to that?

MOSES: You.

AARON: Me!?

MOSES: He told me to take you, that you would be his speaker.

AARON: To Egypt?

MOSES: To our people.

AARON: *(As if realizing the validity of Moses' statements and calling, no longer protesting.)* And when do we go, Moses?

MOSES: Immediately. *(MOSES begins exiting the staging area.)*

AARON: *(Following MOSES, then hesitating.)* Moses, I'm concerned, perhaps even a bit frightened.

MOSES: Trust, Aaron. Trust in our God.

AARON: *(Looking heavenward)* That is all we can do, Moses, trust in our God. *(MOSES and AARON exit the staging area.)*

SCENE 3

AT RISE: The MAGICIAN enters the staging area, proclaiming:

MAGICIAN: His royal majesty, servant of Aton, god of creation and life, Pharaoh Ramses II.

PHARAOH: *(He enters the staging area, quite majestically as befitting his station and position in Egyptian life. Then, from his throne in the front of the staging area:)* **Anubis?**

MAGICIAN: Yes, your majesty?

PHARAOH: I wish a report on the treasure cities.

MAGICIAN: *(Unrolling a scroll, then reading)* **Pithom, treasure city to the east in the land of Goshen, almost completed. Ramses, treasure city to the north in the Nile delta, delayed.**

PHARAOH: Almost completed? Delayed?

MAGICIAN: Yes, your majesty.

PHARAOH: *(Sharply, very sternly)* **Why?**

MAGICIAN: I am only the court magician, your majesty, not the empire's construction expert.

PHARAOH: But you know everything.

MAGICIAN: Not quite everything. *(GERAH enters from the rear of the staging area.)*

GERAH: Your cities, O great Pharaoh, need more laborers.

PHARAOH: More laborers?

GERAH: Yes, my Pharaoh.

PHARAOH: And how would you know, Gerah?

GERAH: I have just come from there.

PHARAOH: From the treasure cities?

GERAH: From Pithom.

PHARAOH: I didn't know you were there.

GERAH: Forgive me, O great and magnificent Pharaoh, but there is much in your kingdom you do not know.

PHARAOH: *(Aggravated by this remark.)* **Silence!**

MAGICIAN: But, Great One, Gerah is correct.

PHARAOH: That my treasure cities need more laborers?

MAGICIAN: Yes.

PHARAOH: But one hundred thousand slaves are already working on my treasure cities and my pyramids.

GERAH: And I fear, O majesty, you will cross the River Styx before ever seeing the completion of either your treasure cities or your pyramids.

PHARAOH: But the slaves have been working for almost twenty years!

GERAH: Your Hebrew slaves have been working at the task, but more must be done to demand they complete this construction!

PHARAOH: More? And what would you have me do?

MAGICIAN: It is not wise to go to war, O Pharaoh, to acquire more conquered peoples for slaves.

GERAH: I say it is. O Great One, your might and the might of Egypt is well known and feared throughout all the world. Our chariots can push to the east, then to the south, and we can conquer more peoples, and thus, more slaves to build to the glory of Pharaoh Ramses II.

MAGICIAN: Egypt's armies are strong, but —

GERAH: *(Sharply)* Egypt has never been defeated!

MAGICIAN: We are not strong enough to build the treasure cities, the pyramids, and wage war at the same time.

GERAH: *(To the PHARAOH)* Egypt did not rise to power being weak!

MAGICIAN: I tell you Egypt is not strong enough to wage war, build the treasure cities, construct the pyramids, and take more slaves! Slaves which we will have to support!

PHARAOH: But I want this construction done! I want my treasure cities and my pyramids completed! Now!

GERAH: And so it shall be done.

MAGICIAN: It is not possible —

PHARAOH: Not possible? For me? The embodiment of all power on earth?

MAGICIAN: *Embodiment* is only a symbol, O Great One. Waging war demands strength.

GERAH: Which I have!

PHARAOH: And I want my eternal home completed before my life is!

MAGICIAN: You have long to live, O Pharaoh.

PHARAOH: *(Correcting his MAGICIAN)* I have forever! I have forever to live! And I wish to spend my forever life grandly in pyramids built to my liking while I am yet alive on this earth to do something about them.

MAGICIAN: If it would please your majesty, what is it you wish changed within the pyramids or the treasure cities?

PHARAOH: I wish them finished! So let it be written, so let it be done!

MAGICIAN: *(Capitulating even while turning, exiting the staging area.)* As your loyal servant, I will determine if Egypt is able to get more slaves.

PHARAOH: We will invade.

GERAH: Whom?

PHARAOH: Our neighbors.

GERAH: No.

PHARAOH: No! A moment ago you were just about to order my chariots into the south and to the east!

GERAH: Our neighbors already pay heavy tribute to you, O Pharaoh. We do not need their sons to build your tomb.

PHARAOH: Across the Red Sea then.

GERAH: There, across the Red Sea, is only desert, dry barren land holding only burning hot sand and camels!

PHARAOH: Then?

GERAH: I have a plan ... meant for the ears of the Great One only.

PHARAOH: And your plan?

GERAH: As your majesty's adviser, I suggest you force the Hebrew slaves to work harder.

PHARAOH: Work harder?

GERAH: Demand more work of them! Force them to do more, more than they have been doing! Teach them what is truly the might of the Pharaoh of Egypt! Demand they give all of their energies to build your magnificent treasure cities!

PHARAOH: But they might die.

GERAH: If they sweat more! Hardly! O great Pharaoh, they are strong. Some among your guards would say *too strong* for the armies of the Pharaoh to handle. They are many; we are few. Work them harder, mighty Pharaoh!

PHARAOH: This is a demand I shall consider.

GERAH: So let it be written, so let it be done. *(The MAGICIAN enters the staging area.)*

MAGICIAN: A messenger, O Pharaoh.

PHARAOH: A messenger?

MAGICIAN: He says he is ordered to speak to you.

PHARAOH: Ordered? By whom? About what? *(MOSES, followed by AARON, enters the staging area.)*

MOSES: I am Moses.

PHARAOH: Moses?

MOSES: Commanded by the Lord God Jehovah.

PHARAOH: The Lord God Jehovah?

MOSES: The God of Israel. And we come with this message:

AARON: "Let my people go, for they must make a holy pilgrimage out into the wilderness, for a religious feast, to worship me there."

PHARAOH: Is that so? And who is this Lord God Jehovah that I, the Pharaoh of Egypt, should listen to him and let Israel go? I do not know this Lord God Jehovah, and I will not let Israel go!

MOSES: The God of the Hebrews has met with us.

AARON: We must make a three days' journey into the wilderness and sacrifice there to Jehovah our God.

PHARAOH: Who do you think you are? These Hebrew people are my slaves building my magnificent treasure cities.

MOSES: Building your graves!

PHARAOH: Get out of my sight! Your people, my slaves, shall not be let go!

AARON: Much trouble shall come to Egypt because of your cruelty.

GERAH: Force the Hebrew people to work harder, O Pharaoh, even as I have suggested. These slaves are idle. I have been there. I have seen what happens. I have seen the slaves singing while they work as if they were attending a banquet! Singing while our Pharaoh's great eternal home remains unconstructed! No, Great One, do not even permit the people of Israel time to listen to the likes *(Pointing toward MOSES and AARON)* of them!

MOSES: As my brother, Aaron, has already said, much trouble shall come to Egypt —

AARON: — because of your cruelty.

MOSES: Great plagues shall come to Egypt.

PHARAOH: You do not threaten me.

MOSES: The Lord God Jehovah —

PHARAOH: Nor your desert god! Get out of my sight! *(MOSES and AARON exit the staging area.)*

PHARAOH: *(Turning to GERAH)* A new command! Do not give the people of Israel any more straw for making the bricks! And do not reduce the quota of bricks to be made by a single brick!

These people obviously don't have enough work

to do or else they wouldn't be talking about going out into the wilderness and sacrificing to their god.

Load these Hebrew people with more work and make them sweat . . . that will teach them to listen to this Moses. *(The PHARAOH exits the staging area as GERAH proclaims:)*

GERAH: So let it be written, so let it be done.

SCENE 4

AT RISE: The MAGICIAN and GERAH move to different sections of the staging area, speaking simultaneously.

MAGICIAN: Pharaoh sends a message to all Egypt: "Increase the hardship on Israel!"

GERAH: *(Hands on hips as a symbol of Egyptian might and power.)* Our mighty Pharaoh commands the Hebrew slaves receive no more straw, but you will continue to make the bricks required of you! But without straw! And you will make more bricks! Pharaoh's pyramids will be built!

MAGICIAN: No Egyptian shall help in any way an Israelite slave. The penalty for doing so is death!

GERAH: Your hours of toil shall be increased! Those slaves fainting under the whip shall be killed! *(These remarks by both the MAGICIAN and GERAH are repeated several times as both the MAGICIAN and GERAH move throughout the staging area. MOSES and AARON enter another section of the staging area even as the MAGICIAN and GERAH continue their proclamations. The PHARAOH also enters another section of the staging area as he is accosted by MOSES.)*

MOSES: I come to you again, O Pharaoh. Let my people go!

PHARAOH: Your people are not *your* people, Moses. Your people are *my* people!

MOSES: You saw the power of my God when I cast my shepherd's rod before your feet, and it became a serpent.

MAGICIAN: *(From the section of the staging area where he is making his proclamation)* A trick which I myself also performed, O Great One. My rod also became a snake.

MOSES: But your snake was devoured by mine!

PHARAOH: I will not let my slaves go!

MOSES: Now you will see again what the Lord God Jehovah's power is! Let the water of Egypt be turned to — *(THOTMES runs into the staging area, shouting:)*

THOTMES: Blood! Father —

PHARAOH: *(Recognizing his son)* Thotmes.

THOTMES: Father, the water has been turned to —

MOSES: Blood! Throughout all of Egypt!

MAGICIAN: A trick! The Pharaoh's magicians have done this kind of trick for hundreds of years!

PHARAOH: Then, I will not let your people go, Moses!

MOSES: Great plagues shall come to Egypt. Hordes of frogs so vast you will not be able to see land. They will come out of the rivers and fill your homes!

MAGICIAN: And we shall do the same, but our frogs will devour yours!

PHARAOH: Get out of my sight!

MOSES: *(As MOSES and AARON are exiting the staging area)* The Lord God Jehovah shall —

PHARAOH: Perish under the might of the Pharaoh of Egypt! *(GERAH moves closer to PHARAOH, re-emphasizing his demands.)*

GERAH: Force the Hebrew people to work even harder, O Pharaoh. The slaves must not listen to these wild men.

PHARAOH: Perhaps we should kill this Moses and Aaron.

GERAH: No.

PHARAOH: No?

GERAH: Let them destroy themselves. As these *supposed* plagues come upon us, we force the Hebrews to work even harder. Then, as their toil becomes more difficult, their punishment more severe, they will soon turn on their Moses and Aaron who have brought even harder and harsher plagues on them through the wrath of Pharaoh Ramses II.

PHARAOH: So let it be written —

GERAH: So let it be done.

SCENE 5

AT RISE: PHARAOH and GERAH move to different sections of the staging area as MOSES and AARON also enter the staging area, each individual utilizing a different section of the staging area.

MOSES: Pharaoh hardened his heart and would not let my people go. This is what the Lord says: "Let my people go so that they may worship me. If you refuse to let them go, I will plague your whole country with frogs. The Nile will teem with frogs. They will come up into your palace and your bedroom and onto your bed, into the houses of your officials and on your people, and into your ovens and kneading troughs. The frogs will go up on you and your people and all your officials."

GERAH: But our magicians also brought frogs to Egypt by their secret, mysterious arts.

PHARAOH: Pray to your God to take the frogs away from me and my people, and I will let your people go to offer sacrifices to the Lord. *(The MAGICIAN [or GERAH] can sing the traditional spiritual "Let My People Go," providing emotional background and tenor to the scene even as MOSES continues to speak.)*

MOSES: But when the frogs were removed from Egypt, Pharaoh again hardened his heart and would not let my people go. This is what the Lord says:

"Let my people go so that they may worship me. If you do not let my people go, I will send swarms of flies on you and your officials, on your people and into your houses. The houses of the Egyptians will be full of flies and even the ground where they are.

"But on that day I will deal differently with the land of Goshen where my people live; no swarms of flies will be there so that you will know that I, the Lord, am in this land.

"I will make a distinction between my people and your people. This miraculous sign will occur tomorrow."

And the Lord did this. Dense swarms of flies poured into Pharaoh's palace and into the houses of his officials and through Egypt the land was ruined by the flies. *(AARON sings a song or chorus of praise as MOSES continues to pronounce judgment upon Egypt.)*

Lice, locusts, and flies filled the air of Egypt,

      choking life in every form and direction.

             Boils festered on the bodies of the Egyptians.

             A hailstorm ruined what crops the vast hordes of locusts had not already devoured, and a heavy ominous darkness covered the earth.

             And yet Pharaoh hardened his heart and would not let the people of Israel go.

GERAH: Perhaps it would be wise, O Noble One, to consider letting the children of Israel go.

PHARAOH: Never!

GERAH: But the destruction that has come upon us —

PHARAOH: Is only for a moment! Egypt has survived much worse! *(THOTMES enters the staging area, walks to and stands beside PHARAOH. The PHARAOH standing by his son, is very determined, very much the ruler.)* I will not permit my son to see his father, Pharaoh of Egypt, weakened. No, the people of Israel shall not leave Egypt while I, Ramses II, am Pharaoh!

MOSES: The Lord God Jehovah will send just one more plague to Egypt. About midnight, the angel of death will pass through Egypt killing the firstborn of every family unless the blood of a lamb is splayed on the lintel of your doorway. The wail of death will resound throughout the entire land of Egypt — *(THOTMES falls at PHARAOH's side, dead.)* — never before has there been such anguish, and it will never be again!

PHARAOH: *(Startled, alarmed, angered.)* **My son . . . is dead. Bring Moses to me.** *(PHARAOH picks up his fallen son, and carrying him, exits the staging area. The MAGICIAN addresses the audience as if speaking to MOSES.)*

MAGICIAN: The God of Moses and of Israel has proven his power. Sing people of Israel! Sing praises to your God! Sing alleluia to your God!

MOSES: Let this night be remembered forever in Israel! The night when the Lord God Jehovah showed forth his power to the Egyptians, passed over us, and brought us out of the land of bondage with mighty miracles. May all the people praise God.

PHARAOH: *(From the rear of the staging area)* **Leave us,**

Moses. Go! All of you. Take your flocks and your herds and be gone. But give us your blessing when you go for we are all as good as dead. *(PHARAOH exits the staging area.)*

MOSES: Let the exodus begin! And in the future when your children ask you, "What is this all about?" You shall tell them, "With mighty miracles Jehovah brought us out of Egypt from our slavery with great power."

MAGICIAN: *(Pronouncement)* So let it be known that on this last day of the four-hundred-thirtieth year of Israel's being in Egypt, the children of Israel, followers of the Lord God Jehovah, are now permitted to leave Egypt *(Pause)* free men. I, Ramses II, Pharaoh of Egypt, do declare it. *(With great finality)* So let it be written, so let it be done.

SHADRACH, MESHACH, AND ABEDNEGO
(Daniel 1; 3)

During the sixth century BC, Nebuchadnezzar, despotic king of the huge and sprawling Babylonian Empire, thirsted for even more power. With his astrologers and advisers, he plotted to expand his power base by invading and defeating countries bordering his empire. The lands and people he conquered became slaves to his wishes and dictatorial rule.

Nebuchadnezzar sent his massive armored armies into the tiny country of Judah, whose people could offer only small resistance. Nebuchadnezzar's armies quickly conquered and subjugated Judah.

To weaken this tiny country for a hundred years into the future, Nebuchadnezzar ordered his armies to bring 25,000 captives to Babylon. Those selected for captivity within the Babylonian Empire had to meet several criteria. First, they were to be male youths, ages eight to fourteen, and secondly, they were to be only the most intelligent, healthiest, strongest, and most attractive Hebrew boys.

Once in Babylon, these Hebrew youths, under careful guidance and continuous scrutiny, would be transformed into

Babylonians. Their proud captors forced them to use a new language, a new dietary regimen, new clothing, customs and traditions, and a new religion.

Very quickly the Babylonians met resistance among these children. Their early childhood training would not permit their food or their religion to be changed or altered in any way. A test of wills and a test of religious faith ensued that would bring the might of the Babylonian king against the power of the invisible God of these Hebrew youths.

CAST OF CHARACTERS

NEBUCHADNEZZAR
King of Babylon
ASHPENAZ
Adviser to Nebuchadnezzar
FIRST ASTROLOGER
SECOND ASTROLOGER
Advisers to the king
SHADRACH
MESHACH
ABEDNEGO
Hebrew youths brought as captives to Babylon
SOLDIER
Servant to the king
ANGEL
A fourth individual in the furnace, described in
Scripture as "looking like a son of the gods"

Note: The roles of First Astrologer, Second Astrologer, Ashpenaz, and the Angel, though traditionally male, can be either male or female characters.

This dramatization could be enhanced by creating two set pieces: a large golden image of King Nebuchadnezzar and a fiery hot furnace, though the production can be, and often has been, staged without either.

Period music could also be utilized to enhance the theatricality of this biblical dramatization.

Scriptural background for this dramatization: *Daniel 1, 3.*

Length of this dramatization: 35 minutes.

SCENE 1

AT RISE: ASHPENAZ, loyal and most faithful servant and adviser to King Nebuchadnezzar, walks proudly into the staging area, then turns and addresses the audience as if everyone within the audience were now conquered subjects of his royal Babylonian master.

ASHPENAZ: People of Judah, today King Nebuchadnezzar, ruler of the powerful Empire of Babylon, proclaims the defeat of your King Jehoiakim.

In claiming this victory for his Imperial Majesty King Nebuchadnezzar, I, Ashpenaz, do now inform you that today and forever more your country of Judah is and will be considered part of the Babylonian Empire. You join an empire whose boundaries encompass most of the world.

Without question, you will obey and follow King Nebuchadnezzar's every wish and his every order. And I, Ashpenaz, am charged with the responsibility of making certain you do.

People of Judah, do not cause trouble for us, and we, representing the might and power of Babylon, will not cause trouble for you. This, as King Nebuchadnezzar's personal envoy to you, I pledge.

King Nebuchadnezzar has today also ordered me to take twenty-five thousand Hebrews into captivity.

I am to select your finest young men to return with me to Babylon, there to become Babylonians, there to serve our mighty and noble king.

Those selected to go to Babylon will be those boys from among your children judged to be the most healthy as well as the strongest, handsomest, and most intelligent! Those youths selected for this privilege of serving our great king will be taken immediately to Babylon where they will begin training and conditioning to be worthy as new "Babylonians." And they will never return to Judah again. *(ASHPENAZ claps his hands, thus ordering a SOLDIER to force into the staging area three Hebrew youths: SHADRACH, MESHACH, and ABEDNEGO.)*

SOLDIER: *(Bellowing as he pushes the three Hebrew YOUTHS into the staging area.)* **Bow! Humble yourselves before King Nebuchadnezzar's chief adviser!** *(No visible response from SHADRACH, MESHACH, and ABEDNEGO, which angers the Babylonian SOLDIER, who shouts:)* **Bow, I said!**

ASHPENAZ: *(Observing the SOLDIER's actions, he becomes quite patronizing of the Hebrew YOUTHS.)* **Please . . . King Nebuchadnezzar begs to be your friend, and I personally extend the king's friendship to you.**

SOLDIER: **I am told these three are among the most intelligent in Judah.**

ASHPENAZ: **Fine! Excellent! Well done, soldier. What are your names?** *(Again, no response from SHADRACH, MESHACH, and ABEDNEGO.)*

SOLDIER: *(Bellowing his anger)* **Your king's adviser asked you a question! Answer him!** *(Still no response from the Hebrew YOUTHS.)*

ASHPENAZ: *(Endeavoring to be diplomatic, yet still possessing a patronizing air and attitude.)* **King Nebuchadnezzar offers you the finest Babylonian hospitality. Nothing will be spared for you. You will be trained in our customs. You will learn of the finest thoughts and ideas in all the world because you will learn the Babylonian way of life. So, don't be afraid of me or your new king. Now, what are your names?**

SHADRACH: **Hananiah.**

MESHACH: **Mishael.**

ABEDNEGO: **Azariah.**

ASHPENAZ: *(Pondering these names)* **Hananiah, Mishael, Azariah . . . good Hebrew names, but unfortunately they are not Babylonian. However, we shall change that . . . now! You will become Babylonians, you must have Babylonian names. As adviser to the king, I rename you Shadrach, Meshach, and Abednego.** *(Each YOUTH struggles to say his new name.)* **With your new names, you will also eventually learn a new language, our language, and you will be given new homes, new clothing, new customs, all Babylonian, and, of course, you will worship new gods, our gods.**

SHADRACH: **That is not possible.**

ASHPENAZ: Not possible?

SHADRACH: We are not able to worship new gods.

ASHPENAZ: And why not?

SHADRACH: We already worship the true and only living God.

ASHPENAZ: The true and only living God? In your opinion only, I assure you.

SHADRACH: The Lord God Jehovah of Judah is our God.

ASHPENAZ: Of Judah? You are no longer "of Judah!" Therefore, this God of yours — whoever or whatever he is — no longer matters. You are now "of Babylon." *(During the next several lines, the SOLDIER exits the staging area, permitting ASHPENAZ to handle these YOUTHS on his own.)*

MESHACH: We may now be "of Babylon," but the Lord God Jehovah will still be our God.

ASHPENAZ: Your God does not go beyond Judah's borders.

ABEDNEGO: But he is the creator of the universe.

ASHPENAZ: And I am chief adviser to King Nebuchadnezzar, and as chief adviser to King Nebuchadnezzar am charged with a responsibility. I say you will worship the gods of Babylon.

SHADRACH: The Lord God Jehovah has given us a law.

MESHACH: You shall have no other gods before me.

ASHPENAZ: Well, the King of Babylon gives you a new law: you shall worship the gods of Babylon.

SHADRACH: That we cannot do.

ASHPENAZ: If you want to live —

MESHACH: Even if we do not.

ASHPENAZ: *(Startled)* What?

ABEDNEGO: We cannot worship another god even if that would mean our deaths.

ASHPENAZ: From this day forward, you are no longer Hebrews! You are now Babylonians, and you will do as commanded in Babylon!

SHADRACH: You may say we are now Babylonians, but that is only an outward appearance, which is something you have changed. But within us, we are Hebrew and that you cannot change. We will never worship idols or false gods.

MESHACH: We will worship only the true and living God.

ABEDNEGO: The Lord God Jehovah.

SHADRACH: No matter where we are.

MESHACH: No matter what you do to us.

ASHPENAZ: We shall see, children, when you get to Babylon and when you come face to face with the greatest power on this earth. I think then your God, whoever he may be, will pale in your sight.

SHADRACH: That will never happen.

ASHPENAZ: We shall see, but permit me to remind you: King Nebuchadnezzar does not take too kindly to those who enjoy the privilege of residence within his empire but do not obey his laws.

SHADRACH: Then permit us to remain here.

ASHPENAZ: That is a request I have no authority to fulfill. Yours is a weak and conquered country, now subject to the laws of your conqueror. Now, come. It is time we were off to Babylon. *(ASHPENAZ, SHADRACH, MESHACH, and ABEDNEGO exit the staging area.)*

SCENE 2

AT RISE: The SOLDIER proclaims the entrance of KING NEBUCHADNEZZAR.

SOLDIER: His Royal Highness, ruler of all Babylon, King Nebuchadnezzar. May King Nebuchadnezzar live forever! *(KING NEBUCHADNEZZAR enters with two advisers, the FIRST and SECOND ASTROLOGERS.)*

KING NEBUCHADNEZZAR: And my army, how will it fare tomorrow against the King of Moab?

FIRST ASTROLOGER: Your armies will succeed. The stars tell us this. The position of the sun and the moon last evening made plotting our charts very interesting. It is generally agreed —

KING NEBUCHADNEZZAR: Among whom?

FIRST ASTROLOGER: Among your finest astrologers.

KING NEBUCHADNEZZAR: *(Apparently lacking total confidence with his ASTROLOGERS)* Astrologers! Huh! Lazy stargazers who think they can tell me how to run my empire.

SECOND ASTROLOGER: It is possible, O Noble One.

KING NEBUCHADNEZZAR: I suppose so . . . to those of us who are so superstitious.

SECOND ASTROLOGER: Not superstitious, King Nebuchadnezzar, wise! We who study the stars are very wise.

FIRST ASTROLOGER: And we become even wiser when we follow what the stars tell us to do!

KING NEBUCHADNEZZAR: Do you think I listened to the stars when I claimed a great victory over Judah? And how is Judah? *(ASHPENAZ enters the staging area just in time to hear KING NEBUCHADNEZZAR's questions. ASHPENAZ responds, quite forcefully, quite proudly.)*

ASHPENAZ: Judah is fine, O Great One. The country is now under your firm control.

KING NEBUCHADNEZZAR: And the captives?

ASHPENAZ: We have brought to Babylon twenty-five thousand captives, just as you commanded.

KING NEBUCHADNEZZAR: Fine. Excellent.

ASHPENAZ: And among them three of Judah's wisest young men for service within your palace.

KING NEBUCHADNEZZAR: Three of Judah's smartest youths? Well, I must see them.

ASHPENAZ: And certainly, you shall, O Majesty. *(Claps his hands; SOLDIER leads SHADRACH, MESHACH, and ABEDNEGO into the staging area.)* **From Judah . . . for King Nebuchadnezzar: Shadrach, Meshach, Abednego.**

KING NEBUCHADNEZZAR: Ah, Babylonian names. *(Quite pleased.)* **So, already you are becoming Babylonian.** *(Looking the YOUTHS over)* **Abednego. How old are you, Abednego?**

ABEDNEGO: Fourteen.

KING NEBUCHADNEZZAR: And do you like Babylon, Abednego?

ABEDNEGO: I'm trying to like Babylon.

KING NEBUCHADNEZZAR: I see, and have my guards been mistreating you, Abednego?

ABEDNEGO: No, not exactly.

KING NEBUCHADNEZZAR: Then, what is it that you

don't like about our empire?

ABEDNEGO: Your food.

KING NEBUCHADNEZZAR: Our food! Well, Abednego, you are in Babylon now. You will have to learn to like Babylonian food.

ABEDNEGO: But Hebrew food would make us healthier!

KING NEBUCHADNEZZAR: Really?

ABEDNEGO: Yes.

KING NEBUCHADNEZZAR: Well, we'll see about that. Ashpenaz, see that they are given Hebrew food. Then, I will watch to see if you do become stronger, my Abednego. *(Pausing a moment to consider and ponder his next statements, then)* So, you three are the smartest young men in all of Judah? We shall see about that, too. Study hard here in Babylon. Learn all you can so you can be a great help to our empire. *(Turning to his ASTROLOGERS)* Wouldn't they be a great help? *(Both FIRST ASTROLOGER and SECOND ASTROLOGER slowly nod their heads in a half-hearted agreement.)* Perhaps I shall test your wisdom now. Shadrach, tomorrow my armies are going to do battle with Moab. What will be the outcome?

FIRST ASTROLOGER: *(Snapping quickly)* That's impossible for this Hebrew youth to answer!

SECOND ASTROLOGER: Not even our study of the stars has fully confirmed what will happen tomorrow with your armies. How can this boy tell you?

KING NEBUCHADNEZZAR: This boy might become one of my advisers some day! Besides, he is supposed to be one of the wisest youths in Judah.

FIRST ASTROLOGER: Wise does not mean prophetic, O King.

KING NEBUCHADNEZZAR: *(Ignoring the words of the FIRST ASTROLOGER)* Tell me, Shadrach, what will happen to my armies?

FIRST ASTROLOGER: Again, I say, he can't possibly know. He doesn't understand the stars.

KING NEBUCHADNEZZAR: Sometimes, I think neither do you!

SHADRACH: Your armies are very large.

KING NEBUCHADNEZZAR: *(Very proudly)* **Naturally.**

SHADRACH: **Too large.**

KING NEBUCHADNEZZAR: *(Affronted)* **Too large?**

SHADRACH: **Too large for the most effective control by your generals. Your army needs more discipline. Your generals should be stronger. They should plan far better strategy.**

FIRST ASTROLOGER: **You would listen to this nonsense from a child?**

SECOND ASTROLOGER: **And from a child whose entire country has been made our subjects, our conquered servants?**

KING NEBUCHADNEZZAR: **Yes, Shadrach, strong words from a country so gloriously defeated by my armies ... and so easily defeated.**

SHADRACH: **My country was weak, small children playing before a great and well-armored giant.**

FIRST ASTROLOGER: **The stars forecast our empire's great victory.**

SHADRACH: **You forecast what King Nebuchadnezzar wanted to hear. You knew King Nebuchadnezzar wanted to be told his armies would be victorious.**

KING NEBUCHADNEZZAR: **I quite agree with you, Shadrach.** *(Turning to address his astrologers directly)* **You see, he is already wise, just as Ashpenaz has said.**

SHADRACH: **Judah's forces were weak, O King. Moab is not. I strongly counsel you to build more strength, more discipline into your soldiers.**

KING NEBUCHADNEZZAR: **Shadrach, what you are saying is correct.** *(Turning back to once again address his advisers.)* **And why could you not tell me these things?**

FIRST ASTROLOGER: **In the future, we will study the movements of the planets with more diligence, O Noble One.**

SECOND ASTROLOGER: **In the future, we will provide you with even more information. Then, you can make wiser decisions.**

KING NEBUCHADNEZZAR: **In the future, my empire may not be here if I rely completely upon your judgments. Shadrach, Meshach, and Abednego, because of your wisdom, I appoint you my personal** advisers. Whenever I need to make important decisions, I will seek your advice and opinions.

FIRST AND SECOND ASTROLOGERS: But ... but ... but?

KING NEBUCHADNEZZAR: *(Turning to appease his ASTROLOGERS)* And I will consider your opinions, also! But, from this day forward, I will also include among my advisers Shadrach, Meshach, and Abednego.

SHADRACH: Our wisdom is from the Lord God Jehovah.

KING NEBUCHADNEZZAR: From whom?

SHADRACH: From the Lord God Jehovah, the true and only living God.

KING NEBUCHADNEZZAR: Yes, yes, I'm sure he is, but in Babylon, we have different gods.

SHADRACH: You have idols, gods made of wood and stone, fashioned by the hands of your own people.

MESHACH: Your gods have hands that are useless, feet that don't move, mouths and ears that aren't able to talk or hear.

KING NEBUCHADNEZZAR: And your God? Is he so different?

SHADRACH: We did not make our God, but rather our God made us! And we can worship no other god, but the Lord God Jehovah. So it is commanded.

KING NEBUCHADNEZZAR: Well, perhaps someday you can tell me more about your God. But at this moment, I have more important matters. I must speak with my generals about your ideas, Shadrach. *(Issuing an order)* Soldier, take Shadrach, Meshach, and Abednego to rooms here in my palace. See that they are comfortable. *(SHADRACH, MESHACH, and ABEDNEGO exit, following the SOLDIER. The KING addresses ASHPENAZ.)* Ashpenaz, you have served me well today, and for this fine and most loyal service, you shall be rewarded ... greatly. And now, come along with me, we must talk to our generals. *(As they together exit the staging area)* Good day, my fine astrologers.

FIRST ASTROLOGER: And what do we do now? This is a turn of events we hadn't planned on —

SECOND ASTROLOGER: And not the best for us either!

Should these youths from Judah rise too high in our government, it could mean the end of us!

FIRST ASTROLOGER: That will not happen!

SECOND ASTROLOGER: That must never happen!

FIRST ASTROLOGER: And I will see that it does not, ever!

SECOND ASTROLOGER: But how?

FIRST ASTROLOGER: I have a plan.

SECOND ASTROLOGER: A plan?

FIRST ASTROLOGER: And it involves Shadrach's God. *(As they are exiting the staging area)* Shadrach says he will worship no other god. Let's see if he really means that! *(Both ASTROLOGERS laugh wickedly, enjoying the thought of planning the downfall of these Hebrew youths.)*

SCENE 3

AT RISE: SHADRACH, MESHACH, and ABEDNEGO enter the staging area as if together in a room in KING NEBUCHADNEZZAR's palace. As they enter, they could be spontaneously singing a chorus of praise or repeating a praise psalm expressing confidence in the delivering power of the Lord God Jehovah.

MESHACH: Hananiah, throughout our history, the Lord God Jehovah has always watched over us as a people.

SHADRACH: Yes, many times.

ABEDNEGO: When?

SHADRACH: When!

ABEDNEGO: I'm afraid here, Hananiah. I'm not as strong as you. I feel lost, lost within a huge foreign empire.

MESHACH: Because we are.

SHADRACH: But not lost to God's sight. Remember Joseph? The young brother given a coat of many colors by his father, a coat which brought to him not only warmth and protection from the sun's rays but also the jealousy and enmity of his brothers!

ABEDNEGO: But Joseph was —

SHADRACH: No different than us, Azariah. He too was carried off into captivity, but not by conquerors. His own brothers sold him into slavery to the camel caravan who in turn sold him into the service of the Pharaoh of Egypt. And what happened?

MESHACH: He became a ruler in Egypt.

SHADRACH: Yes, because he did not forget our Lord God Jehovah. And Moses, remember Moses?

ABEDNEGO: Who could forget Moses?

SHADRACH: Of course, no one in all of Israel will ever forget Moses, yet he, too, was often in a position of great danger before the Pharaoh of Egypt.

ABEDNEGO: But Joseph, Moses — these men were great leaders, filled with faith.

SHADRACH: And often times as frightened as we are now.

MESHACH: Then —?

SHADRACH: But they remained faithful to the Lord God Jehovah, even as we must.

MESHACH: But does the Lord God Jehovah even know we're here? Here in King Nebuchadnezzar's palace?

SHADRACH: Yes, of course he does.

MESHACH: But what I mean is ... do you think God even cares that we're captives of the Babylonians?

SHADRACH: Certainly God cares.

MESHACH: Then, why doesn't he get us out of here?

SHADRACH: Perhaps we can serve God better here in Babylon than ever we could back home.

ABEDNEGO: Serve him better here?

SHADRACH: Perhaps God has brought us here for a purpose.

ABEDNEGO: How could that be possible?

SHADRACH: I'm not certain. After all, his ways are not our ways, but perhaps we are here in Babylon to express our faith.

ABEDNEGO: I would rather have been able to express our faith back home in Judah.

SHADRACH: And perhaps we will return to Judah.

MESHACH: But when? Babylon is strong, too strong. We could never leave. We could never escape.

SHADRACH: Then, we will stay, but we will stay as men of faith.

ABEDNEGO: Even if we are frightened boys!

SHADRACH: And don't you think Joseph or David, even Moses were at times frightened? I believe God understands our fears, and somehow I think he can make us strong even in spite of our fears. *(SHADRACH, MESHACH, and ABEDNEGO exit the staging area even as KING NEBUCHADNEZZAR enters, followed by the FIRST and SECOND ASTROLOGERS.)*

SCENE 4

FIRST ASTROLOGER: King Nebuchadnezzar, you are surely the most powerful ruler in the entire world.

SECOND ASTROLOGER: No one can even approach your majesty, your power.

KING NEBUCHADNEZZAR: *(Could he be suspecting something?)* Yes.

FIRST ASTROLOGER: Is it not only fair that everyone throughout all of the Babylonian Empire recognize your greatness?

KING NEBUCHADNEZZAR: They already do.

SECOND ASTROLOGER: Of course, they do. But there could be a way everyone would be certain to express their gratitude to you for being so great and so mighty a king, an expression of gratitude worthy of so great a majesty as my lord, King Nebuchadnezzar.

KING NEBUCHADNEZZAR: Surely, I agree with you, but how?

SECOND ASTROLOGER: *(Indicating FIRST ASTROLOGER)* He has an idea.

KING NEBUCHADNEZZAR: Which is?

FIRST ASTROLOGER: We suggest that everyone throughout the entire Babylonian Empire worship you.

KING NEBUCHADNEZZAR: Worship me!?

FIRST ASTROLOGER: Let us have built a great golden statue of your majesty, a massive likeness of you which people throughout all of your empire will worship —

SECOND ASTROLOGER: God-like.

FIRST ASTROLOGER: This would certainly seal your power not only within the Babylonian Empire but throughout the remainder of the world —

SECOND ASTROLOGER: *(A very real put-down)* **Such as it is outside the Babylonian Empire.**

KING NEBUCHADNEZZAR: Excellent!

FIRST ASTROLOGER: Then we shall order the statue cast in your majesty's likeness immediately!

SECOND ASTROLOGER: And we shall send special envoys and messengers throughout all of your grand empire, O Majesty. All princes, governors, captains of your armies, judges, treasurers, counselors, sheriffs, and every ruler of each province throughout your empire will be told your command.

FIRST ASTROLOGER: *(As if stating KING NEBUCHAD-NEZZAR's command)* **When the trumpets blow, all citizens of the Babylonian Empire will fall flat on the ground to worship the golden statue of our mighty king, the noble and great Nebuchadnezzar.**

SECOND ASTROLOGER: And ... anyone refusing to obey this new law will be immediately thrown into a flaming, fiery furnace.

FIRST ASTROLOGER: As a sign to the entire world, the great and powerful king of Babylon permits no hint of treason from anyone anywhere within the empire.

SECOND ASTROLOGER: Is that not so, my king?

KING NEBUCHADNEZZAR: Yes, yes, it is true. Place my seal upon this proclamation which will indeed make it law. Then, see that everyone in the empire is so informed.

FIRST ASTROLOGER: As always, your wish is our command.

SECOND ASTROLOGER: Our *most earnest* command. *(Both the FIRST and SECOND ASTROLOGER exit the staging area, but before they leave, both turn to seek some clarification from KING NEBUCHADNEZZAR.)*

FIRST ASTROLOGER: Pardon us, O Noble One, but will this command also include the Hebrew youths recently brought to our, *(Correcting himself)* **your empire?**

KING NEBUCHADNEZZAR: *(Without reflecting upon the import of the question)* **Of course. My laws are binding upon everyone within my empire.**

SECOND ASTROLOGER: *(How long they've waited to hear*

such good news!) **Including Shadrach, Meshach, and —**

FIRST ASTROLOGER: Abednego?

KING NEBUCHADNEZZAR: Are they not "Babylonians" now?

FIRST AND SECOND ASTROLOGERS: Yes, of course. Your words have made them so.

KING NEBUCHADNEZZAR: Then, they will obey my new law. They will worship my image.

FIRST ASTROLOGER: But they worship a foreign God, some Hebrew God.

SECOND ASTROLOGER: Some Lord God Jehovah, of whom we know nothing.

KING NEBUCHADNEZZAR: *(Angered; quite powerfully)* Am I king or not king?

FIRST ASTROLOGER: King, your majesty!

SECOND ASTROLOGER: And a mighty king who lives to serve our people.

FIRST ASTROLOGER: But these Hebrews —

KING NEBUCHADNEZZAR: They are no longer "Hebrews!" They are "Babylonians!" They are my subjects!

FIRST ASTROLOGER: Responsible to obey your laws.

SECOND ASTROLOGER: And to receive their just punishments if they don't.

KING NEBUCHADNEZZAR: So I have spoken.

FIRST ASTROLOGER: Then, so it shall be. *(As both FIRST and SECOND ASTROLOGERS exit the staging area)*

SECOND ASTROLOGER: Then, so it shall be. *(As KING NEBUCHADNEZZAR freezes within his position on the stage, the FIRST and SECOND ASTROLOGERS wander throughout the staging area shouting the new proclamation.)*

FIRST AND SECOND ASTROLOGERS: When the trumpets blow, all citizens of the Babylonian Empire will fall flat on the ground and worship the great golden statue of our mighty king, King Nebuchadnezzar. *(This proclamation is repeated several times throughout the staging area, then:)*

FIRST ASTROLOGER: Anyone refusing to obey this new law, our king's law, will be thrown immediately —

SECOND ASTROLOGER: Into a flaming fiery hot furnace.

FIRST ASTROLOGER: No one shall be exempt from the king's new law.

SECOND ASTROLOGER: And every one disobeying the king's new law will be justly punished —

FIRST ASTROLOGER: Even unto death!

SCENE 5

AT RISE: SHADRACH, MESHACH, and ABEDNEGO enter the staging area, standing to one side. They are talking among themselves, discussing the king's new law.

MESHACH: But the command, which is now law throughout all of the Babylonian Empire, says even we must fall flat on the ground and worship this image of King Nebuchadnezzar!

ABEDNEGO: But we cannot do this, what they ask of us.

MESHACH: But we must.

SHADRACH: You shall have no other gods before you — also a law.

ABEDNEGO: God's law.

MESHACH: But Nebuchadnezzar's law is —

SHADRACH: — only a man's law. We must obey God rather than man.

ABEDNEGO: Even if it means —

MESHACH: Our deaths in a fiery furnace?

SHADRACH: We worship the only true and living God.

MESHACH: But we are not home in Judah, we're captive in Babylon.

SHADRACH: And the Lord God Jehovah is with us.

ABEDNEGO: Hananiah, we'll be thrown into a fiery furnace!

SHADRACH: We must be faithful to our God. Surely, you both know we cannot bow down to a statue made by a man's hands. What kind of a god is that?

MESHACH: Yes, Shadrach, we know. A statue is no god. But perhaps we would only be showing respect if we bowed before this statue.

SHADRACH: No.

ABEDNEGO: No?

SHADRACH: *(Quite definite.)* No!

MESHACH: But —

SHADRACH: The Lord God Jehovah will protect us.

MESHACH: But we're captives in Babylon. Why didn't God protect us from being taken captive when we were home in Judah?

SHADRACH: I don't know. I've already told you that. But I do know we must remain faithful to our God. We will not bow down to an idol even if such not bowing down means our deaths.

ABEDNEGO: I'm frightened.

SHADRACH: Our God will protect us.

MESHACH: But how?

SHADRACH: Let him show us. *(Offstage, the sound of trumpets. KING NEBUCHADNEZZAR enters the staging area to observe what happens among his people even as ASHPENAZ enters, shouting a reminder of the recent royal proclamation.)*

ASHPENAZ: People of Babylon, fall on your knees. Prostrate yourself before the great and mighty Nebuchadnezzar, king of all Babylon, master of the world, representative of life here on earth. Fall on your knees, worship our king!

KING NEBUCHADNEZZAR: Ashpenaz, it's happening.

ASHPENAZ: Of course it is. Everyone throughout your empire is falling to their knees worshiping you.

KING NEBUCHADNEZZAR: Truly, I am a most powerful and great king, am I not?

ASHPENAZ: Did you ever doubt that, O Majesty?

KING NEBUCHADNEZZAR: No. *(Both the FIRST and SECOND ASTROLOGERS rush into the staging area, very much disturbed by a sudden turn of events.)*

FIRST ASTROLOGER: King Nebuchadnezzar! May you live forever!

KING NEBUCHADNEZZAR: My name shall.

SECOND ASTROLOGER: But there are those within your empire, O Noble One, who are not obeying your command.

KING NEBUCHADNEZZAR: *What?*

FIRST ASTROLOGER: They are not bowing down to your great golden image.

SECOND ASTROLOGER: They are not worshiping you.

ASHPENAZ: Who even dares to disobey the law of King Nebuchadnezzar?

SECOND ASTROLOGER: Shadrach, Meshach —

FIRST ASTROLOGER: And Abednego.

KING NEBUCHADNEZZAR: *(Turning to ASHPENAZ)* Could this be true?

SECOND ASTROLOGER: We have seen them ourselves, refusing to bow down and worship your great golden image.

FIRST ASTROLOGER: This is disobedience, O Majesty. Disobedience you must not permit lest others ignore your new law.

SECOND ASTROLOGER: And your greatness.

FIRST ASTROLOGER: After all, you are the king!

KING NEBUCHADNEZZAR: Yes, I am the king! And I will not tolerate disobedience within my empire. I am the king, and my greatness is to be worshiped. *(Clapping his hands together, summoning the SOLDIER. SOLDIER enters the staging area.)* Soldier, bring me Shadrach, Meshach, and Abednego. *(SOLDIER moves to the area where SHADRACH, MESHACH, and ABEDNEGO have remained from their previous scene.)*

ASHPENAZ: Your astrologers are correct, O King. You must make an example of Shadrach, Meshach, and Abednego before their disobedience causes others to laugh at your laws and your greatness. *(SOLDIER moves SHADRACH, MESHACH, and ABEDNEGO to the staging area of KING NEBUCHADNEZZAR.)*

KING NEBUCHADNEZZAR: *(Upon seeing the Hebrew YOUTHS)* Shadrach, Meshach, Abednego, is what I am hearing true? Are you refusing to serve my gods? Are you refusing to worship my golden image? Even after I have commanded everyone to worship me!

SHADRACH: As we have already told you.

KING NEBUCHADNEZZAR: As you have already told me what?

MESHACH: We can worship only the true and living Lord God Jehovah.

KING NEBUCHADNEZZAR: Jehovah! You are in Babylon now!

ABEDNEGO: In Babylon, yes, but we shall continue to worship the only true God.

KING NEBUCHADNEZZAR: My gods are not true?

SHADRACH: Your gods are made by men's hands, and like those same men who are their creators, your gods are powerless, only wood, only gold.

KING NEBUCHADNEZZAR: I'll show you how powerless is my god and am I! I will give you one more opportunity to obey my new law. Tomorrow when the trumpets blow, you had better fall down on your knees and worship my golden image.

ABEDNEGO: And . . . if we don't?

KING NEBUCHADNEZZAR: Then, if you don't, I will have you thrown immediately into a flaming, fiery hot furnace. Then, I'll watch your God take care of you!

SHADRACH: King Nebuchadnezzar, we are not threatened by your fiery hot furnace.

ABEDNEGO: Our God is able to protect us.

KING NEBUCHADNEZZAR: Is he now? We shall indeed see. Tomorrow, I warn you.

MESHACH: Even if our God does not deliver us from your fiery hot furnace, we will know he has a purpose.

SHADRACH: And we will never worship false idols or handmade gods.

KING NEBUCHADNEZZAR: Never?

SHADRACH, MESHACH, ABEDNEGO: Never.

KING NEBUCHADNEZZAR: Then I have no choice! Ashpenaz, have the furnace prepared — now. I will not tolerate this disobedience! I'll have you thrown into the furnace now! *(ASHPENAZ moves to another section of the staging area as if to give a command to those slaves and soldiers working near the fiery furnace.)*

FIRST ASTROLOGER: Make certain, O great King, the furnace is very hot.

SECOND ASTROLOGER: You want these disobedient ones to feel your power and to be crushed under your might. They must not escape.

KING NEBUCHADNEZZAR: *Escape?* There is no way anyone could ever escape the furnace! *(Shouting a command)* Ashpenaz, make the furnace seven times hotter than ever it has been! Shadrach, Meshach, and Abednego will never escape, not from this furnace!

ASHPENAZ: *(Shouting)* The fire is so hot, O King, several soldiers preparing it were burned to their deaths by the heat from the outside of the furnace.

KING NEBUCHADNEZZAR: Excellent. Throw them in! *(ASHPENAZ and the SOLDIER throw SHADRACH, MESHACH, and ABEDNEGO into the fiery hot furnace.)* Now we'll see who is more powerful, your Hebrew God or me, the mighty king of Babylon. *(Turning to his ASTROLOGERS)* They will never escape this! Indeed, this is the best way to show all the world my power, my strength.

FIRST ASTROLOGER: Yes, it certainly is.

SECOND ASTROLOGER: The wisest thing you could have ever done, O Great One. *(KING NEBUCHADNEZZAR turns to enjoy the sight of SHADRACH, MESHACH, and ABEDNEGO being consumed by the fire of the furnace, but is startled by what he now sees! Seconds earlier, a fourth individual, an ANGEL of the Lord, somehow entered the furnace.)*

KING NEBUCHADNEZZAR: What? What is this?

FIRST ASTROLOGER: What's wrong?

SECOND ASTROLOGER: What's happening?

KING NEBUCHADNEZZAR: How many were thrown into that furnace?

ASHPENAZ: *(From near the furnace)* Three.

KING NEBUCHADNEZZAR: How many are in that furnace now?

ASHPENAZ: Four!

FIRST AND SECOND ASTROLOGERS: *Four?*

ASHPENAZ: And the fourth looks like . . . like an angel!

KING NEBUCHADNEZZAR: An angel?

ASHPENAZ: I don't understand. They are not even being burned. *(From inside the furnace, SHADRACH, MESHACH, and ABEDNEGO are singing a chorus of praise or repeating a psalm of praise.)*

SECOND ASTROLOGER: And they're singing!

FIRST ASTROLOGER: Singing? Inside a furnace?

KING NEBUCHADNEZZAR: Shadrach, Meshach, Abednego, what is happening? What is going on in there?

SHADRACH: *(From inside the furnace)* The Lord God Jehovah has sent us an angel.

MESHACH: To protect us from your evil fiery furnace!

KING NEBUCHADNEZZAR: No, no, this cannot be true.

FIRST ASTROLOGER: No one has ever escaped from the furnace!

SECOND ASTROLOGER: It cannot be.

KING NEBUCHADNEZZAR: But it is. *(Moving toward the furnace)* Shadrach, Meshach, Abednego, certainly your God, this Lord God Jehovah, is quite powerful ... more powerful than me, king of Babylon. *(Giving an order)* Soldier, lead Shadrach, Meshach, and Abednego out of the furnace! *(SHADRACH, MESHACH, and ABEDNEGO exit the furnace and stand near the king. The king is stunned, contrite.)* Your God did protect you.

ABEDNEGO: As we said he would.

KING NEBUCHADNEZZAR: Your God did send an angel to deliver you from the fire of my furnace.

MESHACH: As we told you he would.

KING NEBUCHADNEZZAR: Your God is surely more powerful than I.

SHADRACH: As we told you he is. *(KING NEBUCHADNEZZAR now turns to the audience and speaks as if formally addressing the people of his empire.)*

KING NEBUCHADNEZZAR: People of Babylon, hear your king. I now proclaim throughout all the Babylonian Empire that the Lord God Jehovah is the only true and living God. For no other God could save Shadrach, Meshach, and Abednego from the fiery furnace. Ashpenaz, have my golden image destroyed. It is as Shadrach, Meshach, and Abednego say, only an idol ... made by the hands of men ... with no power. Let us worship the Lord God Jehovah. *(Everyone Onstage freezes in position as SHADRACH steps forward, looking heavenward, praying praise.)*

SHADRACH: God, thank you. Thank you for sending your angel to protect us from the fiery furnace and help us to continue to worship and praise your name wherever we are. Amen.

ADONIJAH
(The Prince Who Made Himself King)
(I Kings 1)

Born the fourth son of King David by his wife, Haggith, Adonijah was a most ambitious prince, always desiring someday to be proclaimed "King of Israel."

The three brothers born prior to Adonijah and in line for succession to the throne were now dead, either murdered or killed in battle. Thus, Adonijah felt justified in voicing his overzealous desires even as he issued his demands to be named king.

But David, now quite aged and gravely ill, remained king even though confined to his sickbed. Near death, he continued to hold the allegiance of the Hebrew people. He was still very much a legend and hero to the people of Israel.

Adonijah's ambitions drove him to connive a strategy to unite both Israel's army and priesthood behind him in his bid to take the throne of Israel even while his father, King David, yet lived.

The tactless Adonijah, believing he could better serve the people and God of Israel as king, threw a huge banquet during which he foolishly urged those attending the bacchanalian celebration to proclaim him "King!"

Shouts of "Long live King Adonijah" echoed throughout the city, but only for a moment. Nathan, prophet to the Lord God Jehovah, was divinely sent to the palace of the dying King David with a message and command: "Anoint Solomon true king of Israel!"

Even as King David lie dying, he gave his son, Solomon, his blessing.

For a very brief time, Israel had two kings. But when the people of Israel learned the news that the Lord God Jehovah had spoken, they were pleased to honor their true king, Solomon.

Even Adonijah could not ignore that injunction!

Cast of Characters

(As a two-person presentation)

ADONIJAH
Fourth son of King David by his wife, Haggith
ABIATHAR
A Hebrew priest

(As a four-person presentation)

ADONIJAH
Fourth son of King David by his wife, Haggith
ABIATHAR
A Hebrew priest
NATHAN
A Hebrew prophet
SOLOMON
Son of King David, brother to Adonijah

Note: This biblical dramatization can also be performed as a two-person, three-person, or four-person dramatization.

When performed as a two-person dramatization, the individual playing the role of ABIATHAR also plays the role of NATHAN. The role of SOLOMON is eliminated.

When performed as a three-person dramatization, the role of SOLOMON is eliminated.

Scriptural background for this dramatization: *I Kings 1*.

Length of this dramatization: 35 minutes.

SCENE 1

AT RISE: ABIATHAR, the Hebrew priest, walks onto the staging area, turns toward the audience and begins to share from deep within himself.

ABIATHAR: Ah, the quality of mercy! Who among us can ever truly understand *mercy* unless we ourselves have been the recipients of such a wondrous gift? Mine is a story of *great mercy*, made even more wondrous because the mercy shown and the mercy received came from one brother to another brother, from one son who became king, to another son who wanted so very much to be king, indeed even made himself king, if only for a very short period of time. But nevertheless, he made himself king, and in so doing almost brought rebellion to our land, our tiny country of Israel.

You see, long, long ago, when King David was quite old and quite ill, Adonijah — one of King David's sons, but also not the immediate heir to the throne of Israel — wanted very much to be — *(ADONIJAH enters from the rear of the staging area, interrupting ABIATHAR, bellowing quite vociferously and most raucously.)*

ADONIJAH: — King! I want to be king! I will be king! *(ABIATHAR continues to speak to the audience.)*

ABIATHAR: See . . . it is just as I told you. He's a greedy fellow, this Adonijah —

ADONIJAH: My father, David, is too old to be king! He is no longer effective! I have heard rumors again just this morning that he is so ill he can no longer carry out the responsibilities that are his as king. I could!

ABIATHAR: *(Speaking directly to ADONIJAH)* Impossible.

ADONIJAH: Impossible?

ABIATHAR: While David remains king —

ADONIJAH: While David remains king! He is not *king*!

ABIATHAR: He still holds the throne of Israel.

ADONIJAH: He holds nothing! He is too old, too feeble —

ABIATHAR: Silence! King David is still your father.

Show him respect.

ADONIJAH: And you are my priest. Show me respect!

ABIATHAR: When your actions merit such.

ADONIJAH: Be gone from my sight!

ABIATHAR: And let you do a foolish thing?

ADONIJAH: A foolish thing?

ABIATHAR: Shouting that you want to be king even as your aged father clings to his life, is —

ADONIJAH: The truth!

ABIATHAR: And here is another truth, Adonijah! You are fourth in line for the throne of Israel ... fourth in line does not make you heir to David's kingdom. Fourth in line makes you heir to nothing, Adonijah, nothing!

ADONIJAH: Perhaps, but I will have something!

ABIATHAR: No, Adonijah, no you will not.

ADONIJAH: Why should such superior talents be wasted just because of the mere chance of my birth?

ABIATHAR: Superior talents?

ADONIJAH: To govern Israel.

ABIATHAR: Or is it greed?

ADONIJAH: Greed?

ABIATHAR: To make yourself something you're not.

ADONIJAH: *(Shooting back, harshly)* I am a prince.

ABIATHAR: *(Interpreting the situation correctly)* Ah, but not a king, my prince, and truly, never a king.

ADONIJAH: I suppose you think I could not handle being king.

ABIATHAR: Your pride cannot even handle being a prince.

ADONIJAH: Silence!

ABIATHAR: *Truth* never remains silent forever.

ADONIJAH: *Truth?* That I could not be king ... is that your *truth?*

ABIATHAR: You have spoken, not I.

ADONIJAH: A king of Israel must be a strong and mighty warrior, which I am. I will guide my army's chariots into battle and claim the greatest of victories for Israel, for the Lord God Jehovah.

ABIATHAR: Was our Gideon a strong and mighty warrior? *(Remembering from the eons of time long gone by)* No, I don't think Gideon was anything more than a mere youth, who trusted not in his own strength but in God's ... *(Again, remembering from the eons of time long gone by)* **Ah, but I do remember once ... a great and mighty warrior came forth to rescue Israel ... in fact, the strongest warrior yet known to man ... Samson ... and you will remember, my young and foolish prince, was brought down by the subtlest of all tricks.**

ADONIJAH: Save your breath, Abiathar, I want no more history lessons.

ABIATHAR: Then you shall be doomed to repeat the foolish mistakes of the past.

ADONIJAH: *(With much disdain)* Spoken like a priest —

ABIATHAR: *(Bowing, with much respect)* — which I am.

ADONIJAH: *(Not relenting)* But I want to be king.

ABIATHAR: And I might want to be the High Priest in Jerusalem, but there are some things in life destined never to happen. There are times when we must accept life the way life is because our desires will not change what is reality.

ADONIJAH: No! I will not spend the rest of my life a prince when I could be a king.

ABIATHAR: Better to be alive as a prince than dead trying to be a king.

ADONIJAH: But David is almost dead now ... even as we speak, he lies dying, a king no longer feared by his enemies, an old man wheezing his last breaths —

ABIATHAR: — but still a king ... until he takes that last breath! And even in that moment, David will still be king ... He is a legend to our people and a man after God's own heart.

ADONIJAH: But he is dying!

ABIATHAR: No, Adonijah, he is still living!

ADONIJAH: And he lies in my way —

ABIATHAR: No, Adonijah, he stands between you and your own greed.

ADONIJAH: Enough! You will choose to whom you will be loyal: an old, dying man or a young, virile king! Because I will be king!

ABIATHAR: In your eyes only!

ADONIJAH: In my eyes and the eyes of all Israel.

ABIATHAR: How blind is your ambition.

ADONIJAH: *(Walking quickly, strongly away from ABIATHAR)* **And how deaf you are to the cries of the people.**

ABIATHAR: **The cries of the people?**

ADONIJAH: *(Laughing, knowing he has won.)* **Yes, the people . . . the people of Israel. Even now the people of Israel are coming to a banquet.**

ABIATHAR: **A banquet?**

ADONIJAH: **Yes . . . everyone's coming . . . all my brothers, who are King David's sons, as well as all the men of Judah who are royal officials. They have already watched me make a sacrifice at the Stone of Zohelet near En Rogel. They have already heard my plea!**

ABIATHAR: **Truly, Adonijah, you have sealed your own tomb.**

ADONIJAH: **No, I have made my destiny! I have made myself *king!* (** *ADONIJAH moves triumphantly toward the center of the staging area, strutting his newly-found pride, wearing his newly-proclaimed title much as a red badge of courage. ABIATHAR walks slowly, deliberately toward the altar area of the stage. As ABIATHAR kneels, ADONIJAH pulls himself ever taller in false pride.)*

ABIATHAR: **Lord God Jehovah, forgive the foolishness of this youth who would proclaim himself king.** *(Both ABIATHAR and ADONIJAH speak simultaneously, one speaking to the Lord God Jehovah, the other speaking to himself and his subjects, currently found only within his own mind.)*

ADONIJAH: **People of Israel, hear the news —**

ABIATHAR: **Hear my prayer, O Lord God Jehovah —**

ADONIJAH: **I, Adonijah, the son of King David —**

ABIATHAR: **— and know that we, your people —**

ADONIJAH: **— have this day proclaimed myself *king!***

ABIATHAR: **— still countenance you as our leader.**

ADONIJAH: **Receive your new king and know your future is my destiny.**

ABIATHAR: **And that we, your people, still acknowledge you as our true king —**

ADONIJAH: **Together, we shall show the world a new might, a new strength never before known in Israel.**

ABIATHAR: **— and that our anointed king here on**

earth seeks only to fulfill your will.

ADONIJAH: Our enemies shall shudder, their armor bending like the toys of children before our might.

ABIATHAR AND ADONIJAH: Rise up, O men of Israel —

ABIATHAR: — and call upon your God! *(ADONIJAH exits the staging area. ABIATHAR speaks directly to the audience.)*

SCENE 2

ABIATHAR: Now there was in Israel during this time a prophet of the Lord God Jehovah. *(ABIATHAR picks up a cloak, places the cloak around his shoulders, and "becomes" the prophet of the Lord God Jehovah, NATHAN.)* Tell Bathsheba, Nathan, the prophet of the Lord God Jehovah, has come to the palace of her husband, King David, to speak with her. *(ABIATHAR, as NATHAN, walks toward the audience. NATHAN makes a pronouncement.)*

ABIATHAR / NATHAN: Bathsheba, my queen, go in to King David and say to him, "My lord the king, did you not swear to me your servant: 'Surely Solomon, your son, shall be king after me, and he will sit on my throne?' " Why then has Adonijah become king?

But now Adonijah has become king, and you, my lord the king, do not know about it. He has sacrificed great numbers of cattle, fattened calves, and sheep, and has invited all the king's sons, but he has not invited Solomon, your servant.

My lord the king, the eyes of all Israel are on you, to learn from you who will sit on the throne of my lord the king after him.

Have you, my lord the king, declared that Adonijah shall be king after you, and that he will sit on your throne?

Even now, he is eating and drinking with all the king's sons and the commanders of the army. They are shouting: *(From the rear of the staging area, ADONIJAH can be heard shouting.)*

ADONIJAH: Long live King Adonijah! Long live King Adonijah!

ABIATHAR / NATHAN: *(Bending downward as if speaking to an aged, ailing king)* **Is this something my lord the king has done without letting his servants know who should sit on the throne of my lord the king after him?**

ADONIJAH: **Long live King Adonijah! Long live King Adonijah!**

SCENE 3

AT RISE: ADONIJAH enters the staging area, very confident within his new self-proclaimed position.

ADONIJAH: **People of Israel, how good of you all to recognize me, your prince, son of Haggith, wife to David, as your new king. Soon, I shall go with the commanders of your armies, now my armies, and together, we shall show all the world the strength of our courage, the determination of our resolve to become no longer the footstool of our neighbors but truly masters of our own borders. We shall conquer in the name of the Lord God Jehovah, whose name we shall exalt above every name, whose lordship shall be recognized not only in Israel but in all the world.** *(Even as ADONIJAH is proclaiming his new authority, NATHAN, the prophet, walks back to the altar area. He speaks slowly, as if one having much authority. The young prince, SOLOMON, enters the staging area and responds accordingly to ABIATHAR/NATHAN's commands.)*

ABIATHAR / NATHAN: **My lord Solomon, kneel before Zadok, your priest and me, Nathan, the prophet of the Lord God Jehovah.** *(NATHAN cups his hands, then makes a pantomime movement as if "anointing" Solomon king.)* **Before the Lord God Jehovah and as a ministry to all the people of Israel and Judah, I, Nathan, Jehovah's prophet, do anoint you, Solomon, king of Israel.** *(SOLOMON exits the staging area.)*

ADONIJAH: *(Suddenly becoming aware of the "noise" near him)* **What is this? What is happening? Why is there so much noise throughout the city?** *(ABIATHAR throws off the cloak of NATHAN and hurries to the side of*

ADONIJAH.)

ABIATHAR: My lord Adonijah —

ADONIJAH: Ah, finally, you come —

ABIATHAR: Yes, I come, Adonijah, but not to recognize you as king.

ADONIJAH: Ever the hesitant one.

ABIATHAR: Ever the realist. If you were but worthy to be king of Israel, I would most surely serve you as king.

ADONIJAH: *(Indicating with a gesture that ABIATHAR should kneel.)* **Then, do so. Serve me as king.**

ABIATHAR: I cannot do so for it is as I said. You are not king of Israel.

ADONIJAH: I have made myself king of Israel!

ABIATHAR: And Nathan, the prophet, has anointed your brother Solomon, king of Israel.

ADONIJAH: Solomon? But hear the people proclaiming me their king.

ABIATHAR: No, the people are following the pronouncement of King David. They are acclaiming the anointed one as their king ... and that anointed one is Solomon, son of Bathsheba.

ADONIJAH: Solomon — my brother.

ABIATHAR: Solomon — your king. *(ADONIJAH freezes in his position, suddenly realizing his short-lived and self-exalted life as king has ended. ABIATHAR moves toward the audience and speaks, much as one explaining the "events of time.")* **As I said when first we began talking together, "Ah, the quality of mercy" ... a most wondrous gift when you are the recipient — even as Adonijah was recipient.**

Solomon found his foolish brother, Adonijah, in the temple hiding, cowering behind temple furniture, begging for his life — which was granted to him by a mercy-filled brother, now king, and soon to become known as the wisest man in all of Israel.

I, too, Abiathar, Adonijah's priest, also felt the mercy of Solomon, but one wonders what Solomon would have gained by taking his foolish brother's life. After all, ambitious youth is often far too impulsive, far too nearsighted to ever fully understand its own motives and its own greed. But

in showing mercy, Solomon was remembered forever . . . and as long as the Scriptures are read and recited, a childish man who made himself king will also be remembered because a wise man, a better man, expressed mercy, kindness, and understanding.

May you, too, be remembered not by the actions of another such as Adonijah, but rather by your kindness, understanding, and gracious mercy. May your ways be committed to the Lord, your steps ordered by God, and your life will be blessed in the sight of God and man. *(Both ADONIJAH and ABIATHAR exit the staging area.)*

ELIJAH
(I Kings 16:29-18:45)

The Lord God Jehovah within the first two of the Ten Commandments ordained the purity of monotheistic Judaism by stating: "I am the Lord your God, who brought you out of Egypt, out of the land of slavery. You shall have no other gods before me. You shall not make for yourself an idol in the form of anything in heaven above or on the earth beneath or in the waters below. You shall not bow down to them or worship them . . ."

Israel was surrounded by heathen cultures practicing child sacrifice and idolatry in all forms. Heathen people in their ignorance often debased and mutilated their own bodies while praying to deaf, immobile man-made gods. Tiny Israel struggled to remain an independent nation and to maintain the worship of the Lord God Jehovah without polluting its own theocracy. Israel wanted no part of the carnal religious evils of its neighbors.

It was one man who changed that — Elijah!

Ahab, seventh king of Israel, reigning at Samaria from 871-853 BC, was charged with the responsibility of keeping his country politically strong and spiritually pure. Instead, he very quickly plunged his country into a moral and ethical morass.

Marrying outside the boundaries of Israel, which by law was not permitted, Ahab took the beautiful and quite seductive Sidonian king's daughter, Jezebel, to be his wife and Israel's queen. But Jezebel's unhappiness with her new life situation away from her own homeland and her utter contempt for Israel's Judaistic teachings, created a queen zealously eager to corrupt Israel's Judaism. She was most desirous to entice the people of God to worship the graven image of the Sidonian tribal god, Baal.

With little effort, Jezebel soon induced Ahab to forsake his spiritual responsibility as Israel's king. In hopes of pleasing his deceitful and crafty wife, he permitted idols and priests of Baal to enter Israel. As Jezebel gained more influence within the country, she had many of Israel's prophets killed. Many sacred altars to the Lord God Jehovah were also destroyed.

Israel was being led into a heathen and hedonistic quagmire supervised by 450 priests of Baal and 400 priests of the goddess, Asherah. Meanwhile, the God who had delivered Israel out of its great suffering and intolerable bondage in Egypt was being forsaken.

That is, until the prophet Elijah appeared!

Cast of Characters

AHAB
King of Israel, reigning in Samaria 871-853 BC
JEZEBEL
Sidonian wife to Ahab
ETHBAAL
Prophet to the pagan god Baal and priest to Jezebel
ELIJAH
Prophet of the Lord God Jehovah

Note: ETHBAAL, though traditionally a male, can be either a male or female character.

The theatricality of this dramatization can be enhanced through creatively developing several special effects utilized by the priests of Baal and Asherah to mutilate their hands and arms while vigorously praying to their pagan gods during the spiritual competition on Mt. Carmel between the priests of Baal and the prophet of Jehovah.

Scriptural background for this dramatization: *I Kings 16:29-18:45.*

Length of this dramatization: 35-40 minutes, depending upon the ad-libbed remarks of the prophet, Elijah, and the priests of Baal during the spiritual competition on Mt. Carmel.

AT RISE: The prophet ELIJAH enters the staging area, sternly shouting a proclamation, which in reality is much more a reminder to the people of Israel than a command from divinity.

ELIJAH: Hear, O Israel, the Lord our God is one God.
Remember what he, our God, has said: "You should love the Lord your God with all your heart, all your soul, and all your might.

"For I, the Lord your God, have brought you out of the land of Egypt and out of the house of bondage.

"You shall have no others gods before me.

"You shall not make for yourself an idol in the form of anything in heaven above or on the earth beneath or in the waters below. You shall not bow down to them or worship them. For if you do, I shall show you my power." *(Having reminded the people of Israel of their spiritual responsibility to the Lord God Jehovah, ELIJAH exits the staging area as AHAB enters. AHAB walks to his throne, seats himself, and continues talking to himself, quite disturbed.)*

AHAB: No ... this cannot be! No ... I cannot do this! No, I must remember the God of my fathers, the God of Abraham, Isaac, and Jacob. I must remember what the prophets have spoken and have warned. Israel must not become a land of idols. *(JEZEBEL enters the rear of the staging area and continues her whining.)*

JEZEBEL: Ahab ... King Ahab ... don't you care for me?

AHAB: *(From his throne)* Of course I care for you, my queen.

JEZEBEL: Then, permit me to enter the throne room. Permit me to sit beside you as queen of Israel.

AHAB: How I long to make your wish reality, my precious queen, but you are not from Israel.

JEZEBEL: *(Now quite sharply)* I am your queen! And as your queen, I deserve recognition! *(Changing her tone, becoming smoothly deceptive)* Certainly Ahab, my father, King Ethbaal, would be greatly displeased if I were to tell him you were not providing me the honor due me. And, as you so well know, my father, king of the Sidonians, could indeed choose to make

war on Israel — a war your weak army would lose —
if I were but to tell him of your unwillingness to
recognize what is only and rightfully my due!

AHAB: War! I married you in part to keep our two
countries from war!

JEZEBEL: Then complete your marriage contract. Give
me proper respect! Invite me to share your throne.

AHAB: (*Muttering to himself, caught with a self-made
dilemma.*) I am trapped. What can I do? Nothing! I
cannot please my queen Jezebel, my country Israel,
and my God Jehovah. So if I cannot please all, can
I politically afford to please but one? And if I please
one, do I immediately displease the other two?

JEZEBEL: What is your answer, Ahab? Do I share your
throne, the throne of Israel, or do I return home to
my father's palace, a return which will most surely
and certainly very quickly bring Sidonian armies
galloping, their swords unsheathed, into this tiny
country of yours!

AHAB: (*Hearing her, having made his decision*) I will please
you my queen, and I trust my country and the Lord
God Jehovah will understand. (*Quite pleased with his
decision, JEZEBEL walks toward the throne of Israel.*)
Welcome, Jezebel, welcome to the throne of Israel.
Welcome, *Queen* Jezebel.

JEZEBEL: I am glad and most happy to be here. I
deserve this throne. Now, I have only one more
request.

AHAB: One more request?

JEZEBEL: And this request is important to me.

AHAB: I thought your last request was important to you.

JEZEBEL: Yes, it was, but I am unhappy here.

AHAB: Unhappy?

JEZEBEL: I am lonely here.

AHAB: Lonely? With all your servants? With so much
attention lavished upon you? With all the banquets,
all the people here in Samaria? Lonely!

JEZEBEL: Yes, lonely. I need my priests to provide me
company and to teach me about my god.

AHAB: No.

JEZEBEL: (*Stunned*) *No?*

AHAB: No. You are in Israel now. When you came here

to be my queen, you knew we did not worship idols.

JEZEBEL: When I came here to be your queen, I thought I would be respected as queen.

AHAB: And who does not respect you?

JEZEBEL: You.

AHAB: Me?

JEZEBEL: Because if you would respect me as queen, then you would not deny me the opportunity to worship my god —

AHAB: But your god is an idol!

JEZEBEL: And your God is invisible! Nobody can see your God while everyone can touch and hold mine.

AHAB: What good is touching and holding an idol that possesses no power? That makes no difference within one's life whether it does or does not even exist?

JEZEBEL: And your God, whose existence cannot be seen, does make a difference within lives?

AHAB: He has quite often.

JEZEBEL: Really? And I could say the same.

AHAB: But did your idol part and open the Red Sea for my people, the Israelites, to escape from the cruel Pharaoh and their Egyptian taskmasters?

JEZEBEL: A trick I suppose.

AHAB: But very powerful, would you not agree? More powerful than an idol of stone that can be hauled around in a horse cart!

JEZEBEL: I don't care about your God or about his silly laws! I'm lonely here, and I want my priests. Now!

AHAB: We cannot worship foreign idols here in Israel.

JEZEBEL: Who said?

AHAB: Our God, the Lord God Jehovah.

JEZEBEL: I told you, I don't care about your God!

AHAB: Well, I do.

JEZEBEL: I want my god. I demand my god!

AHAB: (Beginning to cave in) Will worshiping this idol of yours make you happy?

JEZEBEL: (Realizing she is about to get her own way; thus, quite coyly) Yes.

AHAB: And will having your priest here to teach you about your idol-god cause you not to be lonely?

JEZEBEL: (Even more coyly) Yes.

AHAB: *(Giving in once again)* **Then . . . I will grant your request. You may invite one and only one priest here, and he may help you worship your idol.**

JEZEBEL: *(Clapping her hands together)* **Thank you, my king.** *(Clapping again, summoning a prophet of Baal)* **Prophet of Baal, show yourself!** *(As if through this pre-arranged gesture by JEZEBEL, the Prophet ETHBAAL suddenly appears in the rear of the staging area.)*

ETHBAAL: Yes, my queen.

JEZEBEL: **You are welcome in Israel, prophet Ethbaal, my priest.**

ETHBAAL: **Good. Good.** *(JEZEBEL leaves her throne, walking toward ETHBAAL.)*

JEZEBEL: **You are to teach me about my god, and together we may worship Baal.**

ETHBAAL: *(Bowing)* **I am pleased, my queen, that I am able to teach you of our god Baal. But** —*(Hesitating)*

JEZEBEL: **Yes, but what?**

ETHBAAL: But I need an image of Baal.

JEZEBEL: **Yes, of course, you need an idol.**

AHAB: No!

JEZEBEL: *(Turning to face AHAB, again stunned.)* **No?**

AHAB: **There will be no idols here!**

JEZEBEL: **But you permitted my priest —**

AHAB: **To teach you, to help you worship, to quiet your cries of loneliness!**

JEZEBEL: **And how can my priest teach me and help me worship my god without my god?**

AHAB: No.

ETHBAAL: My queen, I must have Baal's golden image.

JEZEBEL: Yes, of course.

AHAB: No.

JEZEBEL: I am returning home.

AHAB: Always you threaten me with war.

JEZEBEL: **More than war. Israel's destruction, your country's death.**

ETHBAAL: Please, my queen, Baal knows no governments other than ours.

JEZEBEL: And I am Sidonian.

AHAB: No, you are now Hebrew.

JEZEBEL: **I may be in Israel, but I will never be a**

Hebrew! My priest must have an idol or I shall —

AHAB: *(Giving in again)* Then bring your idol, but only one, and let your one priest teach you how to worship this worthless piece of stone.

ETHBAAL: A worthless piece of stone only in your eyes, King Ahab.

AHAB: In my eyes and the eyes of all the people of Israel.

ETHBAAL: We shall see, Ahab. We shall see.

JEZEBEL: Bring me an idol as quickly as possible, prophet Ethbaal.

ETHBAAL: I will send messengers bearing your command back to your father even today. And those same messengers shall return bearing our glorious god Baal, but — *(Hesitating)*

JEZEBEL: Yes, but what?

AHAB: *(Sensing another request)* No!

ETHBAAL: But where, my queen, shall we place Baal's golden image?

JEZEBEL: Yes, where?

AHAB: No.

ETHBAAL: We must have a temple built in which to worship our god.

JEZEBEL: Yes, of course —

AHAB: No.

JEZEBEL: — a temple must be built.

AHAB: No. No temple.

JEZEBEL: But my priest, prophet Ethbaal, is right. I cannot worship my god unless I have a proper place to do so.

AHAB: No.

JEZEBEL: Would you worship your God just anywhere?

AHAB: We do. We can.

JEZEBEL: Well, I cannot! I must have a temple. Baal must have a temple, a proper place in which to be venerated and worshiped. *(Quite forcefully)* You must build Baal a temple, Ahab!

ETHBAAL: *(As if a fait accompli)* And the temple must be large, very large . . . and in the center of the main courtyard, we will place an even larger statue of Baal so all Israel can see Baal and worship his likeness and know of his greatness.

AHAB: Israel worship Baal? Impossible! Never!

ETHBAAL: *(As if teaching, though in reality correcting AHAB's statement)* The people of Israel will like *seeing* a god, and we can quite easily see Baal.

AHAB: The Lord God Jehovah is most powerful.

ETHBAAL: *(Continuing)* And the people of Israel will like touching Baal's strong arms and hands made of priceless gold.

AHAB: The people of Israel do not need to touch their God to know he exists.

ETHBAAL: *(Continuing)* And the people of Israel will kneel down before Baal, falling prostrate before his greatness because, Ahab, King of Israel, even your people like to see and touch their gods, to feel as if they exist.

AHAB: The people of Israel worship the Lord God Jehovah. They will never worship the idol Baal.

ETHBAAL: Your people will change, Ahab. When they see Baal's beautiful golden image and can enter his magnificent temple, the people of Israel will compare a great and beautiful Baal to an invisible Jehovah, and then, they will worship Baal, a god they can see and touch.

AHAB: It is against our laws, his command.

ETHBAAL: It may be against your laws or his commands, but your people will do just as I have said. Israel will worship Baal because their eyes will very quickly tell them that Baal is truly greater than something invisible! *(Now speaking directly to JEZEBEL)* Come, my queen, we must supervise the building of Baal's temple. *(ETHBAAL and JEZEBEL exit the staging area.)*

AHAB: *(Muttering to himself)* What can I do? What can I do? *(ELIJAH enters the staging area.)*

ELIJAH: *(Speaking directly to AHAB)* You can obey the Lord God Jehovah! *(AHAB appears shaken by the sudden entrance and admonition of ELIJAH, who continues even as ETHBAAL enters the staging area carrying an idol of Baal, which he places on an altar.)* Israel is not to be made a land of idols.

ETHBAAL: *(Praying to the idol)* O great and magnificent Baal, help good Queen Jezebel and myself, your humble prophet and priest . . . help us to build a great and wondrous temple to your honor and glory here in Israel.

ELIJAH: You see, Ahab! You see what you have permitted to enter the land of Israel! Idols! False gods! First, you married Jezebel, who was not from Israel. Then, you permitted Jezebel to bring an idol and a priest. And now you are permitting a temple to be built to Baal! You have disobeyed the Lord God Jehovah.

AHAB: I did not want to . . . Jezebel made me do it!

ELIJAH: But it was you who disobeyed the Lord God Jehovah! And because you did, I have a message from the Lord God Jehovah for you. God has provided me with insight, and I am to say to you: "As surely as the Lord God of Israel lives, the God whom I worship and serve, there won't be any dew or rain for several years until I say the word!" *(ELIJAH exits the staging area.)*

AHAB: What is happening? No rain! No dew! Oh, that can't be true!

ETHBAAL: *(From his altar to Baal)* Do not worry, my king. Baal will hear the pleas of your people here in Israel. If the land becomes dry, Baal will make it rain.

AHAB: Baal! Baal is no god. Baal is an idol, a piece of stone hewn from rock and carved with your own hands. What kind of a god is that? *(From the rear of the staging area can be heard ELIJAH repeating a psalm of praise to the Lord God Jehovah or singing a chorus of praise to the Lord even as AHAB speaks.)* Your idols must be taken out of Israel, Jezebel! Your statues of Baal must be destroyed!

JEZEBEL: *(Entering another section of the staging area)* No. Never!

AHAB: But it has not rained for months . . . almost a year.

JEZEBEL: Is that my fault?

AHAB: Yes.

JEZEBEL: I haven't caused the rain to stop falling.

AHAB: Your idols have!

JEZEBEL: Ha! I thought you said my idols could do nothing. You said my idols were powerless. Now you say my Baal stops the rain!

AHAB: There is no rain because of your idols.

JEZEBEL: There is no rain because of your Elijah, who has suddenly and very much like a coward disappeared. Find this Elijah and force him to make it rain.

AHAB: But no one knows where Elijah is.

JEZEBEL: You are the king. Find him!

AHAB: Yes, I am the king, and once more, I shall do as you say. I shall send soldiers everywhere searching for Elijah. *(AHAB exits the staging area. JEZEBEL joins ETHBAAL at the altar of Baal. ELIJAH enters the rear of the staging area.)*

(NOTE: The following sequence is best if ELIJAH is not seen but heard by the audience.)

ELIJAH: *(Praying)* God, King Ahab's soldiers are searching everywhere for me. I must find a safer place to remain for some time. Also, God, the stream at which I was drinking ... because it has not rained for more than a year ... the stream has dried up. Please help me.

ETHBAAL: *(Also praying)* Bring rain to the parched earth, O great and magnificent Baal. Bring rain to this barren land. We can no longer stand this drought. We will soon all die.

AHAB: *(Entering the staging area)* It has not rained for a year and a half.

JEZEBEL: *(From the altar of Baal)* Find Elijah!

AHAB: Get rid of your idols!

JEZEBEL: Find Elijah!

AHAB: Israel was not to have anything to do with idols.

JEZEBEL: Find Elijah!

AHAB: The streams are now dry beds of burning hot sand. The animals are dying. Our crops no longer grow.

JEZEBEL: Find Elijah!

AHAB: I have tried to find Elijah. *(Now each character makes a statement.)*

ELIJAH: My soul magnifies the Lord! My spirit rejoices in the Lord! Holy is the name of Jehovah!

ETHBAAL: Bring rain to our land, O great and

magnificent Baal.

JEZEBEL: Find Elijah!

AHAB: Get rid of your idols. Get rid of Baal. *(Then, the above statements are repeated simultaneously by each character three times, building in volume and intensity to a climax over which can be heard the final time ELIJAH's statement: "Holy is the name of Jehovah!" ETHBAAL and JEZEBEL then exit the staging area. ELIJAH then enters the staging area, confronting AHAB and JEZEBEL.)*

ELIJAH: No rain has fallen for three years, King Ahab of Israel.

AHAB: So, it is you . . . Elijah . . . the man who brought this disaster upon Israel. You must do something about what is happening in Israel!

ELIJAH: And what is happening in Israel?

AHAB: Surely you know as well as I do. Everything is dying. We have no food. My people are starving to their deaths. Why have you let this happen to us?

ELIJAH: You are talking about yourself. For you, King Ahab, and your family have refused to obey the Lord and have instead worshiped Baal.

AHAB: I have never worshiped Baal.

ELIJAH: But you have permitted Baal to be worshiped in Israel.

AHAB: By Jezebel!

ELIJAH: That is enough!

AHAB: Why? I am not Jezebel. I am not responsible for what Jezebel does.

ELIJAH: You disobeyed the Lord God Jehovah. You gave permission to have idols and priests brought here and now a temple to be built.

AHAB: But what does that matter?

ELIJAH: Such permission is just the beginning. People will worship the idols of Baal and forget the true God. *(JEZEBEL enters the staging area, immediately confronting ELIJAH, much as if she had been listening to the prophet from a room Offstage.)*

JEZEBEL: If they forget the true God, then how true is he?

AHAB: Jezebel!

JEZEBEL: What good is a god people forget?

ELIJAH: Our God has protected Israel for thousands of

years.

JEZEBEL: But now he sends no rain. Now your God causes you to die!

ELIJAH: As a judgment.

JEZEBEL: A judgment? *(Laughing)* Why?

ELIJAH: It is not good for people to worship idols, mere pieces of wood and stone that can do nothing. Ever! It is not good for people to bow down and pray to such wood and stone or to work hard and give their money to pieces of wood and stone carved into idols.

AHAB: Which god will bring rain? That is what is important now!

JEZEBEL: Yes ... which god can bring rain?

AHAB: That's what we need now! We need rain. Israel must have rain, and I will worship the god that brings rain.

JEZEBEL: And that god will be Baal!

ELIJAH: All right. We shall have a test. Bring all the people of Israel to Mt. Carmel with the prophets of Baal, and we will see whose god is the more powerful.

AHAB: But why should we do this, Elijah?

ELIJAH: How long are you going to waver between Baal and the Lord God Jehovah, Ahab? If the Lord is God, follow him! But if Baal is god, then follow him. *(ETHBAAL enters the staging area, moving toward the section utilized as "Mt. Carmel.")* Because of Jezebel, I am the only prophet of the Lord God Jehovah left. She has had slain all the others, but Baal has four-hundred-fifty priests and prophets! *(Then as if commanding AHAB)* Get two bulls for us! Let them choose one for themselves, and let them cut it into pieces and put it on the wood but not set fire to it. I will prepare the other bull and put it on the wood but not set fire to it. *(To ETHBAAL)* Then you call on the name of your god, and I will call on the name of the Lord God Jehovah. The god who answers by fire is truly God!

ETHBAAL: An apt challenge, Elijah! *(Beginning to pray to Baal, quite loudly)* O Baal, great and magnificent Baal, today is the day to show your strength! Today is the day to send fire from heaven to this altar to

show your great and mighty power!

(NOTE: This prayer can be repeated several times or another similar prayer can be ad-libbed at the discretion of the director.)

ELIJAH: *(Finally)* **Shout louder, priest of Baal. Perhaps your idol cannot hear you!**

ETHBAAL: *(Shouting even louder)* **O Baal, great and magnificent Baal, send fire from heaven!**

AHAB: **There is no fire. There will be no rain.**

(OPTIONAL: Special effect: ETHBAAL making a cut within his wrist.)

ETHBAAL: *(Begging, pleading)* **O Baal, great and magnificent Baal, hear my prayer. I give myself to you, and in turn ask you to send fire from heaven to this altar.**

AHAB: **There is no fire. Nothing is happening.**

JEZEBEL: **Give Baal time.**

AHAB: **How much time? All your four-hundred-fifty priests can do nothing! Baal can do nothing!** *(JEZEBEL shouts: "Give Baal time!" even as ETHBAAL shouts: "Send fire!" This is repeated several times until finally silenced by AHAB.)* **Silence! Baal can do nothing!** *(All characters except AHAB freeze in position. AHAB steps forward, toward the audience. He explains the events that followed.)* **Then Elijah took twelve stones, one for each of the tribes descended from Jacob, and with these stones built an altar in the name of the Lord God Jehovah. And then, while we watched in disbelief, he dug a trench around the altar!**

Having completed this task, he placed wood on top of the altar, took and cut the bull, which he then placed on the wood, and ordered my soldiers to bring water!

Water! Such a precious item as water!

How could we spare water at such a time of drought as this? But my soldiers obeyed the prophet of the Lord God Jehovah and poured water over the altar — three times! — until the altar was drenched

and the trench was full of water!

ELIJAH: *(Stepping from his frozen position, praying)* **O Lord, God of Abraham, Isaac, and Jacob, let it be known today that you are God in Israel and that I am your servant and have done all these things at your command. Answer me, O Lord, answer me, so these people will know that you, O Lord, are God, and that you are turning their hearts back again.** *(ELIJAH returns to his frozen position as AHAB continues to explain the events that followed.)*

AHAB: **Then the fire of the Lord fell from heaven and burned up the sacrifice, the wood, the stones and the soil, and also licked up the water in the trench!**

When all the people saw this, they fell prostrate and cried, "The Lord, he is God! The Lord, he is God!" *(ETHBAAL, JEZEBEL, and ELIJAH exit the staging area.)* **And soon, as truly the miracle it was to all of Israel, the sky grew black with clouds, the winds rose, and a heavy rain came to Israel for which we could only say** *(As he exits the staging area)*, **"Praise to the Lord God Jehovah for the Lord, he is truly God!"**

ESTHER
(Esther)

More than a hundred years after 25,000 Hebrews had been carried into captivity by King Nebuchadnezzar's Babylonian soldiers, many Hebrews remained within the empire. But now the Babylonians had themselves been conquered and their once glorious "Babylonian" Empire had become the harsh and barbarian "Media-Persian" Empire.

Ahasuerus (also known as Xerxes) became king of Media-Persia in 486 BC. To celebrate his ascension to the Media-Persian throne he threw a huge banquet in his own honor in his citadel city of Susa.

All the king's officials, rulers, and representatives from throughout the Media-Persian Empire, which stretched from India to Ethiopia, were asked to attend. The banquet continued for six months during which time King Ahasuerus made a great display of his wealth and power to the power brokers within his empire.

Near the conclusion of this banquet, which was utilized as a means to generate even more support for himself through royal boasting, King Ahasuerus desired to show off his queen.

Traditionally, a king's queen would then be commanded to show herself, often clothed in little or no raiment, to those attending such a banquet.

Vashti, queen to King Ahasuerus, not wanting to so demean herself, sent word to the king's banquet she would not attend such a raucous function.

Her disobedience brought her immediate end as queen of Media-Persia! Thus began an empire-wide search for a new queen, a search that sought beautiful candidates for queen in every village and every city throughout the 127 provinces of the empire.

After the exhaustive search for a new queen, a young and very beautiful Hebrew maiden was selected to become wife to King Ahasuerus and the new queen of Media-Persia. But no one in authority was aware of the new queen's ethnic origin.

During her reign as queen, Hadassah, who assumed the Persian name of "Esther," was challenged by her Uncle Mordecai to save all the Hebrews then living within the Media-Persian Empire from execution.

Haman, ambitious prime minister to King Ahasuerus, had convinced the powerful king that the Hebrews were planning to assassinate him. He suggested that all — every man, woman, and child of Jewish origin in all of Media-Persia — should be executed on the same day. Believing his prime minister, King Ahasuerus commanded the execution of all Hebrews throughout Media-Persia.

The king's command became a law of the Medes and Persians, and as a law, it could never be changed or altered in any way, except by another new law, superceding and negating the previous law.

Esther was begged to intercede on behalf of her people. Any intercession would have to produce a new law of the Medes and Persians negating the already-existing law. This would be very difficult. To intercede, Esther would need to approach King Ahasuerus in his throne room. But to enter the throne room uninvited by the king was tantamount to expressing a desire to physically harm, perhaps even assassinate the king.

Therefore, entering the throne room of the Media-Persian king uninvited was forbidden by law. Penalty: the uninvited intruder's immediate death!

Only an extension toward the uninvited intruder of the king's golden scepter, the symbol of his power and might, by the king himself could spare the intruder's life long enough for the king to hear the reason for such an intrusion.

Esther's courage to approach King Ahasuerus within his throne room uninvited, and her subsequent victory in persuading the Media-Persian king to command into law the salvation of her people, continues to be celebrated each year during the Hebrew holy day known as "Purim."

Cast of Characters

TERESH
Advisor to Queen Vashti
KING AHASUERUS
Despotic king of Media-Persia
HAMAN
Prime minister during Ahasuerus' reign
MORDECAI
Treasurer within the palace of Ahasuerus; a Hebrew
ESTHER
Selected to become the new queen; also a Hebrew

Note: The role of TERESH can be either a male or female character.

Also, the ending of this biblical dramatization could be enhanced with ESTHER and MORDECAI singing together a chorus of praise such as the Hebrew chant, "Hava Nagila" or perhaps a more contemporary worship chorus.

Scriptural background for this dramatization: *The Book of Esther*.

Length of this dramatization: 35-40 minutes.

SCENE 1

AT RISE: TERESH enters the front of the staging area and talks to both KING AHASUERUS and PRIME MINISTER HAMAN, who stand near the rear of the stage, perhaps engrossed within a conversation of urgent state importance.

TERESH: She will not come, your majesty!

HAMAN: What?

TERESH: Queen Vashti refuses to attend your banquet!

HAMAN: Did you tell her the king himself commands her presence?

TERESH: Yes, my lord prime minister, and even with my lord the king's command, the queen still refuses to come to the banquet!

AHASUERUS: Refuses me, her king?

TERESH: Yes, your majesty, and Queen Vashti says her mind will not be changed!

HAMAN: You must not let Vashti do this to you, King Ahasuerus! Her refusal to attend your royal banquet, especially this banquet being given in your honor, O majesty, defies your authority. Such defiance could lead to rebellion within your empire.

TERESH: Nonsense!

HAMAN: My lord king, reason with me. Your most loyal governors, generals, and government officials are attending this banquet, even now as we speak. These officials hold much power throughout your empire, and they know you have invited Vashti, your queen, to show herself to them. Unless your wife soon arrives at the banquet tables, you will appear foolish in the eyes of the most powerful men in your empire. They will see you as weak, unable even to control your own wife!

TERESH: Queen Vashti wishes me to assure her husband, the king, her refusal to attend the banquet is not an affront to him, but rather an attempt to maintain her own privacy.

HAMAN: Her own privacy?

TERESH: The queen does not wish to appear at the king's banquet simply to have his men look at her.

HAMAN: But that is Vashti's function as queen!

TERESH: In your eyes, my lord prime minister.

HAMAN: Such disobedience, my king, will surely not go unnoticed by your generals! Again, my king, reason with me. You are the supreme ruler of Media-Persia, and as supreme ruler, your word is law. But once this law is defied — no matter by whom or for what purpose — your rule and your control is no longer supreme. One act of disobedience will beget another act of disobedience and that in turn another. Where will such disobedience end? Perhaps your forced removal from the throne?

AHASUERUS: Never!

HAMAN: Then, your majesty, you must do something about Vashti's disobedience! Or appear to the world a weak child willing to let his throne slip out of his hands!

TERESH: Your majesty, I beg of you — do not be so harsh!

HAMAN: And, King Ahasuerus, I beg of you — do not be so easily influenced by this weak advisor!

TERESH: The queen wishes you no harm —

HAMAN: The queen laughs in your face —

TERESH: The queen wishes only to preserve her personal dignity —

HAMAN: The queen's dignity is preserved when she stands beside her king! But perhaps the queen is plotting rebellion, even now conspiring with other officials, perhaps at your own banquet?

TERESH: Nonsense!

HAMAN: The queen dares to disobey your royal command —

AHASUERUS: Silence!

HAMAN: You are able to silence me, your most loyal prime minister, your majesty, but someday you may not be able to silence the laughter of your queen's conspirators or the sounds of their swords clashing against the shields of your own palace guard.

AHASUERUS: I will be king! Over Media-Persia! And over my wife!

HAMAN: Then, silence not me, your loyal servant, your majesty, but silence your queen, who makes the mighty Ahasuerus appear to be a child who cannot even control his own wife!

TERESH: There is no truth in what Haman says, my king. There is no conspiracy meant in the queen's actions.

AHASUERUS: I will determine if there is conspiracy in my queen's actions!

HAMAN: Well spoken, my king.

TERESH: And I assure you there is none.

AHASUERUS: Then, if there be no conspiracy, let my queen come to my banquet.

TERESH: But —

AHASUERUS: But if she does not come to my banquet hall and specifically to my side at the banquet table, then I will declare Vashti a traitor, and —

HAMAN: Demand her death!

AHASUERUS: Immediately!

TERESH: This is your decree?

AHASUERUS: This is now my law!

TERESH: Then you have sealed the queen's fate.

AHASUERUS: So let it be done.

HAMAN: I shall execute your order at once, my king. All disobedience shall be eliminated.

AHASUERUS: And, Haman —

HAMAN: *(Turning back toward the KING)* Yes, your majesty?

AHASUERUS: Begin the search for a new queen.

HAMAN: Yes, your majesty.

AHASUERUS: Search every city, every village, every home throughout my one hundred twenty-seven provinces and find the most beautiful girl in all my empire. And when that most beautiful girl is found, bring her to me, and I will make her the new queen of Media-Persia! *(Most obediently, HAMAN exits.)*

TERESH: King Ahasuerus, I beg of you — reconsider your decision.

AHASUERUS: *(Exiting the staging area)* My decision is now the law of the empire, a law of the Medes and Persians, which cannot be changed.

TERESH: But Queen Vashti —

AHASUERUS: There is no longer a Queen Vashti! *(Both AHASUERUS and TERESH exit the staging area.)*

SCENE 2

AT RISE: MORDECAI enters the staging area.

MORDECAI: *(Calling)* **Hadassah! Hadassah! Where are you, Hadassah?**

ESTHER: Here, Uncle Mordecai.

MORDECAI: Hadassah, I have news for you!

ESTHER: What news?

MORDECAI: Such good news!

ESTHER: Such good news? For me?

MORDECAI: The king is searching for a new queen!

ESTHER: This is good news for me?

MORDECAI: Of course, Hadassah.

ESTHER: But why is this good news for me, Uncle Mordecai?

MORDECAI: Because you, Hadassah, will be the king's new queen!

ESTHER: Me?

MORDECAI: King Ahasuerus wants the most beautiful girl in all of Media-Persia.

ESTHER: *(With much disbelief)* **And you think that is me?**

MORDECAI: Of course, and King Ahasuerus will think so too.

ESTHER: But I am a Hebrew!

MORDECAI: So?

ESTHER: That means I am not Persian!

MORDECAI: The king's edict doesn't say the future queen must be Persian, but the edict does say he wants every province, every city, every village searched for the empire's most beautiful girl, and not every province in Media-Persia is Persian!

ESTHER: But we are a conquered people, brought to Babylon much as slaves.

MORDECAI: Even more the reason you should go to the king. With you, a Hebrew, as queen our people are safe.

ESTHER: Safe? Safe from what?

MORDECAI: We never know. We Hebrews have been victims of so many kings so often, we should place our own people in high places to better secure our future.

ESTHER: But you, Uncle Mordecai, are already in a high place. You're the king's treasurer.

MORDECAI: Which is indeed an honor, but we truly need you as queen.

ESTHER: I will never become queen.

MORDECAI: How do you know?

ESTHER: I know.

MORDECAI: Have you been to see the king?

ESTHER: No.

MORDECAI: Then, do not say you will never become queen! Hadassah, I beg you — go to King Ahasuerus' palace, see the king, let the king see you —

ESTHER: And if he selects me?

MORDECAI: Then, of course, you shall be queen, queen of Media-Persia, and there will be much rejoicing among our people!

ESTHER: But I am frightened to do this.

MORDECAI: In life, we are often frightened. That is why we have God. So go, Hadassah, see the king.

ESTHER: *(Quietly, calmly)* I will do as you ask.

MORDECAI: But before you go, Hadassah, change your name.

ESTHER: Change my name?

MORDECAI: Why let your Hebrew name tell the king you are from Jerusalem? There are those yet around the king who remember our forefathers were captured by the Babylonians, and to them we are and we shall always be slaves.

ESTHER: But what name shall I choose?

MORDECAI: Esther.

ESTHER: Esther?

MORDECAI: Esther is a Persian name, meaning "rising star," and like a beautiful evening star, you, Hadassah, shall ascend to new heights in Media-Persia.

ESTHER: God willing.

MORDECAI: God willing. Now, go my child, see the king.
(Both ESTHER and MORDECAI exit the staging area.)

SCENE 3

AT RISE: KING AHASUERUS enters the staging area quite

disturbed, pacing, and through his pacing expressing his frustration, even his anger.

AHASUERUS: Have I seen every candidate for queen in my empire? And none, not one of them, beautiful enough, fine enough to be my queen!

Are there no more possibilities for my queen? Have I seen every beautiful girl in Media-Persia? From over my vast empire which stretches from India to Ethiopia, there is no one fine enough to be my queen? *(At this distressing news, AHASUERUS seats himself on his throne, sullen, depressed, angered.)*

TERESH: *(Entering from the rear of the staging area)* Yes, O great King Ahasuerus, there is yet someone else to be considered for your queen.

AHASUERUS: What?

TERESH: There is yet someone else to be considered for your queen.

AHASUERUS: Well, where is this someone else? Bring her to me at once! I must see her!

TERESH: Yes, your majesty. *(Motioning ESTHER to enter the staging area)* King Ahasuerus, permit me to present to you — Esther.

AHASUERUS: Esther? *(AHASUERUS stands, moves away from his throne and toward ESTHER, who stands silently beneath the leering gaze of the king.)* Ah, yes, Esther ... you are indeed a beautiful girl ... possibly even the most beautiful girl in all of Media-Persia ... and you shall be, even as your name indicates, a "rising star" in all of Media-Persia because I shall make you my queen. *(He extends his hand in a welcoming gesture.)* Queen Esther.

HAMAN: *(Entering the staging area, quite disturbed.)* King Ahasuerus ... King Ahasuerus —

AHASUERUS: Yes, my lord Haman?

HAMAN: A most urgent matter!

AHASUERUS: Yes, my lord prime minister?

HAMAN: *(Seeing ESTHER)* A matter demanding your immediate attention, my king!

AHASUERUS: *(Realizing HAMAN is questioning ESTHER's presence)* My lord prime minister Haman, this is Esther, whom I shall very soon make the new queen of Media-

Persia. *(HAMAN bows most respectfully.)* **And this, Esther, is Haman, prime minister of Media-Persia, second only to me in power and authority throughout my empire.** *(ESTHER bows most respectfully.)* **And now, Esther, Haman has an urgent matter, which he desires to discuss with me. I regret I have not more time for you at this moment, but surely you can search out this, your new home, my palace, and return to me at a more convenient time.**

ESTHER: Yes, my lord king. *(ESTHER bows, again most respectfully, and exits the staging area with TERESH, who perhaps will serve as guide to the new resident of the palace.)*

AHASUERUS: And now, Haman, what is this urgent matter?

HAMAN: A plot to assassinate you has been discovered here in your palace.

AHASUERUS: What?

HAMAN: Yes, your majesty. Your treasurer, Mordecai, has heard news of a conspiracy to overthrow your rule and in overthrowing your rule to also end your life.

AHASUERUS: Who is involved within this conspiracy? I demand to know! I demand to be told!

HAMAN: Several of your own advisors, my king.

AHASUERUS: My own advisors!

HAMAN: Obviously, they perceive you to be weak, even as I said this might happen, and in that weakness, these plotting advisors suspect your throne has become vulnerable, theirs for the taking.

AHASUERUS: Never!

HAMAN: I have already had these treacherous and traitorous advisors imprisoned —

AHASUERUS: Good.

HAMAN: — waiting only for you to seal their fate.

AHASUERUS: Death.

HAMAN: *(Bowing most respectfully)* But of course.

AHASUERUS: *(As he exits the staging area)* Immediately!

HAMAN: Consider these traitors executed, my king. *(Upon AHASUERUS' exit from the staging area, and thus from his throne room, HAMAN finds himself enjoying a sense of a newly-acquired power through the destruction of this plot against the king. He speaks to himself, almost too confidently.)* **Truly, I am becoming a most powerful**

man in Media-Persia, perhaps in all the world.
Certainly, someday everyone throughout Media-
Persia will bow down to me, their lord.

MORDECAI: *(From the rear of the staging area)* **That will
never happen, Haman!**

HAMAN: *(Startled)* **What?** *(Then angered.)* **What was that?**

MORDECAI: **You will never become the most powerful
person in all the world.**

HAMAN: *(Said with much disgust)* **Mordecai . . . what do
you know about that?**

MORDECAI: **I know you desire power too much! And
that overzealous desire will find you in great trouble
someday.**

HAMAN: *(Defending himself for no readily apparent reason)*
**The king has entrusted me with great responsibility
throughout all his empire.**

MORDECAI: **But of course.**

HAMAN: *(Recovering his composure; becoming arrogant.)* **So,
you should be falling down on your knees bowing
to me, grateful I let you even live.**

MORDECAI: **I should be bowing to you?**

HAMAN: **As is everyone else in this empire.**

MORDECAI: **Why?**

HAMAN: **Why?**

MORDECAI: **Yes, why?**

HAMAN: **Because I am the prime minister of Media-
Persia, second only to the king himself in power and
authority throughout this great empire. I deserve
honor; I deserve your respect. You and people like
you should bow to me.**

MORDECAI: **I will never bow to such an evil greed for
power, Haman.**

HAMAN: **What?**

MORDECAI: **For in my bowing to you, I pay homage to
your corrupt ambitions and your ill-gotten gain.**

HAMAN: **Well, Mordecai, we shall see about this! You
will bow to me!**

MORDECAI: **Never.**

HAMAN: **Never?**

MORDECAI: **As I have said.**

HAMAN: **And as I have said,** *(Exiting the staging area, quite
angry)* **you will bow to me.**

MORDECAI: *(Calling his niece)* **Esther! Esther!**

ESTHER: *(Entering)* **Yes, my uncle.**

MORDECAI: **You have become the new queen of Media-Persia!**

ESTHER: **So I have been honored —**

MORDECAI: **With a very great responsibility from our God.** *(Both ESTHER and MORDECAI exit the staging area.)*

SCENE 4

AT RISE: HAMAN and KING AHASUERUS enter. HAMAN is trying to persuade KING AHASUERUS of his worth. Throughout this time of persuasion, HAMAN has an ulterior motive, which he quite skillfully masks from KING AHASUERUS.

HAMAN: **King Ahasuerus, am I not prime minister?**

AHASUERUS: **But, of course, you are, Haman. You know that, why ask such a foolish question?**

HAMAN: **And have I not served you faithfully as your prime minister?**

AHASUERUS: **Another foolish question? Of course, you have served me faithfully, most faithfully.**

HAMAN: **And am I not second in power and authority throughout all the empire?**

AHASUERUS: **Haman, again, why even ask?**

HAMAN: **Because I have great concern for your reign as king.**

AHASUERUS: **Great concern?**

HAMAN: **O my king, once more there are people in your empire who despise you and wish you ill and are this very moment plotting against you.**

AHASUERUS: *What?*

HAMAN: *(Fiendishly)* **These people are scattered throughout your kingdom. Their laws and ways are different from those of our nation, and they refuse to obey your laws.**

AHASUERUS: **Refuse to obey my laws?**

HAMAN: **These people do not deserve to live in a land you so benevolently rule, O king.**

AHASUERUS: **Who are these people?**

HAMAN: I am grieved that I must be the one who always carries such tragic news to you.

AHASUERUS: Who are these people?

HAMAN: That I must be the one who hears and then reports evil traitorous plots against you, my friend —

AHASUERUS: And you, my lord Haman, are also my trusted friend. Who are these people?

HAMAN: You must rid our empire of these evil people forever! I suggest that on one day you rid the empire of all Jews!

AHASUERUS: The Jews?

HAMAN: Yes, they are traitors, secretly conniving against you, and let us, O majesty, teach not only the Jews but all the world a lesson about your strength and Persian justice! On one particular day, decreed by you, have your soldiers kill every man, woman, and child throughout all of Media-Persia who is a Jew.

AHASUERUS: Every Jewish man, woman, and child? But what have these people done wrong?

HAMAN: *(Very treacherous)* Rather what *will* these people do wrong?

AHASUERUS: But an entire people? Certainly an entire people cannot plot against me!

HAMAN: Do not even say that, my king!

AHASUERUS: But for what reason do they plot against me?

HAMAN: Ingratitude for your graciousness to them. I am told the Jews are even whispering plots with our neighbors.

AHASUERUS: Who gave you this information?

HAMAN: A wise prime minister has eyes and ears everywhere.

AHASUERUS: And a wise king?

HAMAN: Responds to the concerns of his prime minister. Destroy these Jews —

AHASUERUS: But an entire people!

HAMAN: — before they destroy you.

AHASUERUS: Once before, you told me of a plot to assassinate me, and then I wisely believed you and you were right. The traitors were found. So now, even though I find what you are telling me most

difficult to accept, I will heed what you say. *(Within two different areas of the staging area, two scenes are happening simultaneously: MORDECAI confronts ESTHER; HAMAN confronts KING AHASUERUS.)*

MORDECAI: Esther, you must do something.

ESTHER: What? What, Uncle Mordecai, can I do?

HAMAN: I suggest, O great king, that you publish an edict, a new law, stating that on one particular day every man, woman, and child who is a Jew should be killed.

AHASUERUS: But such a strong edict!

MORDECAI: Go to the king! Tell the king what Haman is saying is not true.

ESTHER: But Haman is the prime minister!

HAMAN: It only takes one knife to end your life.

AHASUERUS: But an entire people because of one knife?

MORDECAI: And you, Esther, are the queen!

ESTHER: With no power!

MORDECAI: But you are close to the ear of the king.

HAMAN: Who knows which of those people might wield the knife that claims your life?

AHASUERUS: Publish the law throughout all of Media-Persia.

ESTHER: But it has been a very long time since the king has called for me.

MORDECAI: You must go to him!

HAMAN: All Jews shall be killed?

MORDECAI: You must save our people!

AHASUERUS: Yes. All Jews shall be killed.

ESTHER: But —

HAMAN: No exceptions?

AHASUERUS: One exception and that exception, as you have said, might be the very one who thrusts the knife into me. Destroy all the Jews!

MORDECAI: Esther, you must save our people!

HAMAN: Your decree shall become law and be made known throughout all the empire. I shall see to this new law myself. *(AHASUERUS exits. HAMAN "publishes" the new law throughout the empire. He walks throughout the staging area, proclaiming:)* **Within the month, every man, woman, and child who is a Jew**

shall be killed. *(HAMAN states this law several times in several different areas of the stage.)*

ESTHER: Our death is now law!

MORDECAI: Which only you can change.

ESTHER: No, Uncle Mordecai, the law of the Medes and the Persians can never be changed!

MORDECAI: No, Esther, King Ahasuerus can decree a new law which could put an end to his first evil decree.

ESTHER: But would he?

MORDECAI: Only if you persuade him the Jews wish him no harm.

ESTHER: That will be very difficult.

MORDECAI: But it is your responsibility . . . before God. It is for this moment, Esther, that God has brought you to the throne of Media-Persia.

ESTHER: You believe that, Uncle Mordecai?

MORDECAI: Yes.

ESTHER: But the king has not asked for me. I have not even seen Ahasuerus for months!

MORDECAI: Esther, are you not also a Jew?

ESTHER: Yes.

MORDECAI: Do you think you will escape?

ESTHER: No one knows I am a Jew.

MORDECAI: Haman has spies everywhere. He will soon know. His hatred of me runs too deeply —

ESTHER: His hatred of you?

MORDECAI: Yes, it is because of me that Haman has plotted against our people.

ESTHER: You?

MORDECAI: I would not bow down to his evil greed nor to him.

ESTHER: Then you go to King Ahasuerus!

MORDECAI: To enter the king's throne room without being summoned means —

ESTHER: Death.

MORDECAI: Yes.

ESTHER: But it is the same: death for you or death for me if I enter the king's throne room without his summons.

MORDECAI: But, Esther, should the king extend his golden scepter, then you will be granted audience and live!

ESTHER: And you think the king will extend his golden scepter toward me?

MORDECAI: Much more quickly to you than toward me.

ESTHER: But you are his treasurer!

MORDECAI: Whom he never sees, and you are his queen!

ESTHER: Whom he hasn't seen too often.

MORDECAI: Esther, the king loves you. His love for you will extend the scepter.

ESTHER: *(Slowly)* Then, I will go to King Ahasuerus in his throne room, and if I perish, I perish.

MORDECAI: I pray God will save us through you.

ESTHER: Have all the Jews in the palace and in the empire pray for three days. Then, I will go to see King Ahasuerus. *(ESTHER and MORDECAI exit.)*

SCENE 5

AT RISE: HAMAN and KING AHASUERUS enter the staging area.

HAMAN: *(Quite pleased with himself.)* **The law has been sent to every province within your mighty empire, O great king, and this new law demanding the death of all the Jews has been greeted with much approval and great enthusiasm.**

And I myself have been overseeing the construction of a gallows here near the palace for that day when every Jew shall be killed.

I have had this gallows built, O great king, so that you may see the faces of your traitors as they walk to the gallows, knowing their plots have been exposed, knowing their evil conspiracies ended even as their very wretched lives shall be ended!

AHASUERUS: *(Seating himself on his throne)* **You have done well, my lord Haman.**

ESTHER: *(Appearing from the rear of the staging area)* **King Ahasuerus?**

AHASUERUS: *(With much disbelief)* **Esther?**

ESTHER: *(With some timidity)* **King Ahasuerus, I, your queen, would ask the pleasure of an audience with you.**

HAMAN: *(Concerned)* You know the law, Esther. No one without a royal summons approaches the king in his throne room.

ESTHER: But, my lord prime minister Haman, anyone may be recognized by the king.

HAMAN: Death is —

ESTHER: Already close to me, my lord Haman.

AHASUERUS: What?

ESTHER: My great king, I request the pleasure of an audience. *(Slowly, cautiously, KING AHASUERUS extends his golden scepter toward ESTHER.)*

AHASUERUS: You have that audience, Esther.

ESTHER: I must discuss a matter of extreme urgency with you.

AHASUERUS: What matter?

HAMAN: What could be so urgent from you?

ESTHER: Tonight, my king, I will host a banquet for you and my lord prime minister Haman. Then, during the banquet, I will discuss this urgent matter with you.

AHASUERUS: I shall be there.

ESTHER: And my lord prime minister, will you be there?

HAMAN: To attend a banquet hosted by you, Esther, my queen, will indeed be an honor.

ESTHER: But, my lord Haman, please know the honor is all mine. *(ESTHER exits the staging area.)*

AHASUERUS: What could be so urgent a matter that Esther risked death to enter my throne room?

HAMAN: I am not certain, your majesty. I am not certain. *(HAMAN and KING AHASUERUS walk to another area of the stage which serves as ESTHER's own banquet room. In the minds of the characters, some time passes during this blocked movement to ESTHER's banquet room.)*

SCENE 6

AHASUERUS: Ah, Esther, certainly this has been a splendid banquet, but now you must tell me what is the urgent matter you wanted to discuss with me?

HAMAN: Yes, my queen, tell us what is of such urgent

and so much importance to you.

AHASUERUS: Please, Esther, I am intrigued with your mystery. Tell me how I can be of help to you, and I will give whatever it is you want, even up to half of my kingdom!

ESTHER: If I have found favor with you, my king —

AHASUERUS: But, of course, you have.

ESTHER: And if it pleases your majesty —

AHASUERUS: Anything ... yes ... anything ... ask, and it shall be granted you.

ESTHER: Then grant me my life!

AHASUERUS: Your life?

HAMAN: Who threatens the life of our queen? Tell us so I can immediately end this evil, vicious plot against my queen!

ESTHER: I am doomed to destruction.

AHASUERUS: Impossible!

HAMAN: Quickly, tell us who conspires against you, my beautiful queen!

ESTHER: *(Most emphatically)* **You!**

AHASUERUS: Haman?

HAMAN: Me?

ESTHER: He has convinced you, my king, and wrongly, that my people are plotting to destroy you and your kingdom.

AHASUERUS: Your people?

ESTHER: My lord king, I am a Hebrew. My Hebrew name is Hadassah. Mordecai, your treasurer, is my uncle.

AHASUERUS: But your people are plotting my death!

ESTHER: My people have enjoyed prosperity here within Media-Persia with you as their king. None of my people wish you harm.

HAMAN: This is not true, my king!

ESTHER: What you have said, Haman, is not true! You have demanded the deaths of an innocent people because of your own greed and evil ambition.

AHASUERUS: What?

ESTHER: My king, Haman lied about my people because one Jew would not bow down and fall prostrate in front of him.

AHASUERUS: One Jew would not bow down to Haman?

HAMAN: I tell you, my king, this is not true. Esther speaks —

AHASUERUS: Silence!

ESTHER: Mordecai refused to bow to Haman.

AHASUERUS: Mordecai?

ESTHER: Yes.

AHASUERUS: And why should Mordecai bow down to you, Haman?

ESTHER: Mordecai is also a Jew, a Jew who has proven his loyalty to you not only by serving you so faithfully for many years but also saving your life from an assassination plot, my king.

AHASUERUS: Yes, I remember.

HAMAN: What she says is not true!

AHASUERUS: Esther risked death to come to my throne room without a royal summons. Only truth could command such courage!

HAMAN: But the Jews are wicked, evil traitors!

AHASUERUS: No, it is you, you Haman who are wicked, you who desire power, you who plot to gain even more power. Perhaps you plot against me even now!

HAMAN: But I am your prime minister!

AHASUERUS: No! You were my prime minister! From this moment on, Mordecai will be my prime minister, and you, Haman, you shall be executed on the very gallows that you had built for Mordecai. Your own lying greed shall be your end!

HAMAN: But —

AHASUERUS: Esther, I shall change the law! Your people shall be spared and never will I make such a decree again.

ESTHER: Thank you, my king. *(From the rear of the staging area MORDECAI can be heard rejoicing, quite grateful, "Thank you, Lord God Jehovah.")*

Section II

AUDIENCE PARTICIPATION DRAMATIZATIONS

*(These plays can also be effectively
performed without audience participation.)*

The following four dramatizations — *Gideon, Naboth's Vineyard, Daniel in the Lions' Den* and *Jonah* —include "audience participation," thus providing an opportunity for members of the audience to become spontaneously involved within the actual re-telling of the biblical account.

Throughout the scriptings of these dramatizations will be suggestions detailing how to involve various members of the audience within specific sections of the play.

This involvement is best when spontaneous and totally unrehearsed. To involve the audience in such a manner, the actor playing the role necessitating audience participation simply moves toward the audience, suggests his or her need for assistance at this point, asks individuals from the audience to become involved, and subsequently involves those audience "volunteers" within the action of the dramatization as described within the play's script.

Such spontaneous involvement is enjoyed by individuals of all ages and not only adds a "new" dimension to the dramatization being staged, but also assures that those audience members participating within the dramatization will better understand and learn the message of the biblical account because they were "a part" of its re-telling.

Depending upon the performance situation, the audience could be told during a brief opening introduction of the opportunity for spontaneous participation within the dramatization.

However, "spontaneous" audience participation should be just that: immediate and unrehearsed involvement and participation by audience volunteers or those specifically selected by the actor needing such involvement at the moment when such involvement is necessitated.

GIDEON
(Judges 6:1-7:25)

The Israelites often found themselves victims of their more powerful neighbors. The Old Testament account found in *Judges,* tells how Israel was confronted yearly for seven years by the Midianites. Their army was so strong and oppressive that the Israelites were forced to seek shelter in mountainous caves when the Midianites came to ravage their crops and lands.

The Midianites, together with the Amalekites and other savage peoples to the east of Israel, regularly charged into Israel's grain fields taking not only the harvested grain but also livestock, sheep, and donkeys.

For seven harvests, the Israelites endured this devastating invasion described in Judges 6:5 as being like "swarms of locusts" devouring the land! Finally, in their agonizing and hungering distress, the Israelites cried out to the Lord God Jehovah, begging his intervention, seeking some divinely created relief.

Then suddenly, an angel of the Lord appeared to a youth threshing wheat in a wine press, hoping to keep this grain hidden from the Midianites.

The youth, Gideon, was startled!

He was told that he would defeat the mighty Midianite armies!

Disbelieving the angel represented the Lord God Jehovah, Gideon pleads his total unacceptability for such a major militaristic task. He considered himself the least and weakest member of a family that he believed to be the least among the families of his tribe, which in turn was the least in all the twelve tribes of Israel! He — Gideon —fight the Midianites? Impossible!

But after testing the angel of the Lord, he came to realize that the Lord God Jehovah, not he himself, would be the power to defeat the Midianites.

Cast of Characters

GIDEON
A youth from the tribe of Manasseh
ANGEL OF THE LORD
A representative of the Lord God Jehovah

Scriptural background for this dramatization: *Judges 6:1-7:25*.

Length of this dramatization: 30-40 minutes, dependent upon the audience participation.

SCENE 1

AT RISE: The ANGEL OF THE LORD is at rear of the staging area, unseen but heard:

ANGEL OF THE LORD: I am the Lord your God, who brought you out of Egypt, out of the land of slavery. You shall have no other gods before me. *(GIDEON enters the staging area, rather remorseful.)*

GIDEON: O God, Israel has been at the mercy of Midian for seven years, seven long years of oppression, hardship, and great difficulty. Surely, Israel has sinned.

ANGEL OF THE LORD: *(Continuing unseen but heard.)* You shall not make for yourself an idol in the form of anything in heaven above or on the earth beneath or in the waters below.

GIDEON: Israel's people have forgotten you, and they have sought after iniquity. Without shame or fear, they have clamored for other gods, gods they could see, gods they could hold in their own hands, idols that will look mighty, but in truth, are meaningless carvings, amulets possessing nothing more than superstition, golden molds mirroring Israel's own foolishness.

ANGEL OF THE LORD: *(Continuing unseen but heard.)* You shall not bow down to them or worship them —

GIDEON: Because of this, Israel's sin, your children, my people, have done evil in your sight and truly Israel deserves to be chastized and to be reminded of their creator, their God, who tolerates no idolatry.

ANGEL OF THE LORD: *(Continuing unseen but heard.)* — for I, the Lord your God, am a jealous God.

GIDEON: And thus, the Midianites have been that oppressive chastizement — so much so — that we Israelites have been forced to seek shelter and refuge in caves whenever the Midianites charge into our land.

Each year at harvest, our crops are stolen, and what the Midianites themselves do not steal, their camels eat, trample, ruin. For seven years, always at harvest, the Midianites come upon us like swarms

of locusts, devouring and destroying the crops we
toil so long and so hard to grow.

We, O Lord God Jehovah, are impoverished!
We have nothing. We have nowhere to turn. We have
no one to help us — unless you yourself will do so.
(Kneeling) So, Lord God Jehovah, hear our cries, the
cries of Israel, and become our strength, our shield,
and our defender.

SCENE 2

AT RISE: As GIDEON completes his prayer, the ANGEL OF
THE LORD enters the section of the staging area near
GIDEON, calling the youth's name.

ANGEL OF THE LORD: Gideon! Gideon!
GIDEON: *(With timidity)* **Yes?**
ANGEL OF THE LORD: The Lord is with you —
GIDEON: *(Quietly questioning)* **The Lord is with me?**
ANGEL OF THE LORD: — mighty warrior.
GIDEON: Mighty warrior? Me?
ANGEL OF THE LORD: Yes.
GIDEON: Surely you are mistaken. I am no mighty
warrior.
ANGEL OF THE LORD: Through me, you shall be.
GIDEON: Forgive me, but who are you?
ANGEL OF THE LORD: I am the angel of the Lord.
GIDEON: Of the Lord?
ANGEL OF THE LORD: The Lord God Jehovah.
GIDEON: No . . . I — I — can't believe . . . the angel of the
Lord here on earth . . . appearing to me? *(To himself)*
I am not Abraham, Moses, Jacob. Why would the
angel of the Lord come to me?
ANGEL OF THE LORD: I have chosen you for an
important task.
GIDEON: You have chosen me?
ANGEL OF THE LORD: Yes.
GIDEON: You have chosen me for an important task?
ANGEL OF THE LORD: Yes.
GIDEON: What kind of an important task?
ANGEL OF THE LORD: You shall deliver Israel out of
Midian's hand.

GIDEON: I shall deliver Israel out of Midian's hand. *(Reflecting for a moment)* **I shall deliver** ... *(Suddenly the thought grabs him!)* **I shall what?**

ANGEL OF THE LORD: Evil has invaded Israel, but not as an enemy nor as a stranger. Israel has welcomed this iniquity.

GIDEON: Are you talking about the Midianites?

ANGEL OF THE LORD: No, Gideon, the Midianites are not the evil that has invaded Israel.

GIDEON: *(Understanding)* **Idolatry.**

ANGEL OF THE LORD: Israel has permitted idolatry to flourish within its borders —

GIDEON: *(To himself)* **Israel has not been faithful** —

ANGEL OF THE LORD: — and Israel has fashioned graven images to grace its mantels and kitchen tables.

GIDEON: Baal.

ANGEL OF THE LORD: An idol.

GIDEON: *(Looking heavenward, beseeching.)* **Lord God Jehovah, forgive my people ... for they know not what they do.**

ANGEL OF THE LORD: Israel knows. My law came to them through Moses.

GIDEON: *(As if to provide an excuse)* **But Moses was so very long ago. People forget.**

ANGEL OF THE LORD: My commandments are eternal.

GIDEON: But —

ANGEL OF THE LORD: Have I not sent prophets to Israel continuously to remind my people?

GIDEON: Yes ... *(Again as if to provide an excuse)* **but we have so many prophets. At times it seems every day brings a new prophet, each claiming divine insight. Who can tell which prophet speaks the truth, which prophet truly is sent from God?**

ANGEL OF THE LORD: Try his spirit. Observe the fruit of his message, *(Repeating his previous injunction)* **and the Lord is with you, Gideon, mighty warrior! Go in the strength you have and save Israel out of Midian's hand.**

GIDEON: But, Lord, how can I save Israel?

ANGEL OF THE LORD: I will be with you.

GIDEON: But I am only a youth. I am not strong. I have

no arms other than a thin sword. My family is the least in the tribe of Manasseh, and I am the least in my own family. I do not represent Israel. I don't speak for my people. I speak only for myself, and that, not well. How could I possibly mount an attack against Midian? Who would follow me, a leader with no strength, recognized by no one?

ANGEL OF THE LORD: Man measures strength in military might, numbers of soldiers —

GIDEON: Both of which I do not possess.

ANGEL OF THE LORD: Both I will provide.

GIDEON: Strength?

ANGEL OF THE LORD: Yes.

GIDEON: In me?

ANGEL OF THE LORD: Through me.

GIDEON: Soldiers?

ANGEL OF THE LORD: They will come.

GIDEON: In great numbers?

ANGEL OF THE LORD: In sufficient numbers. If true strength, Gideon, rested in many soldiers, then a tiny seed could never push its way upward through a thick and heavy soil, but it does, and like a tiny seed sprouting heavenward so shall you conquer in my name.

GIDEON: But Midian has thousands of soldiers!

ANGEL OF THE LORD: I will be with you.

GIDEON: When Midian's soldiers come to Israel, their tents and camels cover the ground — so much so — one cannot even see the ground! They are truly like a great plague upon us.

ANGEL OF THE LORD: You will strike down the Midianites as if they were but one man.

GIDEON: If I have found favor in your eyes, then please, please give me a sign so I will know you are really *you*. I mean that you are really the angel of the Lord God Jehovah talking to me. *(At this, the ANGEL OF THE LORD moves to the rear of the staging area.)* Please ... do not go away until I come back and bring my offering and set it before you. *(GIDEON hurries Offstage even as the ANGEL OF THE LORD laments.)*

ANGEL OF THE LORD: O, Israel, Israel, my people.

(From the rear of the staging area, GIDEON speaks.)

GIDEON: I am preparing a sacrifice, a personal offering, from me to you, O Lord God Jehovah. I offer you the meat of a young goat, an ephah of flour made into bread without yeast.

Hear, O Israel, the Lord our God is one God.

ANGEL OF THE LORD: Place the meat and the bread upon that rock over there, and pour the broth over it. *(GIDEON pantomimes the actions commanded by the ANGEL OF THE LORD.)*

GIDEON: *(Astonished)* **My sacrifice has burst into flame of its own accord!** *(If possible, GIDEON enters the staging area carrying a bowl of fire.)*

ANGEL OF THE LORD: Your sacrifice is acceptable in my sight.

GIDEON: *(Kneeling, completely in awe.)* **My Lord God Jehovah —**

ANGEL OF THE LORD: Peace.

GIDEON: **— truly I have seen the angel of the Lord face to face!** *(GIDEON now stands, his spirit overflowing with a psalm of praise.)* **I will sing to the Lord, for he is highly exalted. The Lord is my strength and my song; he has become my salvation. He is my God, and I will praise him, my father's God, and I will exalt him. Who among the gods is like you, O Lord? Who is like you — majestic in holiness, awesome in glory, working wonders?**

In your unfailing love you will lead the people you have redeemed. In your strength you will guide them to your holy dwelling. You will bring them in and plant them on the mountain of your inheritance — the place, O Lord, you made for your dwelling, the sanctuary, O Lord, your hands established.

The Lord will reign forever and ever. Sing to the Lord, for he is highly exalted.

ANGEL OF THE LORD: Destroy the wooden idol of the goddess, Asherah, and destroy the altars Israel has built to Baal.

Erect an altar to the Lord your God. Then, I will deliver Midian into your hand, Gideon. *(But suddenly, GIDEON's excitement and mood changes. He appears to be frightened.)*

GIDEON: But God, what you want me to do? To do battle with the Midianites is too difficult. I can't do it. Even as I speak, the Midianites and the Amalekites are joining forces. The soldiers have crossed the Jordan River and have camped in the Valley of Jezreel.

ANGEL OF THE LORD: *(Again unseen but heard.)* **Gather your soldiers together.**

GIDEON: My soldiers? I have no soldiers!

ANGEL OF THE LORD: I will be your strength.

GIDEON: Lord, I'm afraid. I have no strength. I am a thresher of wheat, a tiller of the soil — not a soldier — and certainly never a warrior. I cannot battle Midian ... especially when I don't have courage or confidence in myself.

ANGEL OF THE LORD: You shall not boast in your strength, but in mine.

GIDEON: If you will save Israel by my hand as you promised, I need a sign. A sign! I know I shouldn't doubt. I know my faith should be strong, that fear should be a stranger to me, that my concern should be smothered by my courage, but then I think of Midian, their soldiers, their armor, the destruction they've inflicted upon Israel for seven long years, and I — I need a sign that I will know you are God, that you are with me.

ANGEL OF THE LORD: Your sacrifice.

GIDEON: Yes, I know I had a sign ... once, but that was long ago. I am merely a youth.

Perhaps if I could command a great army, perhaps if I had great forges that melted ore, created iron hammered into heavy weapons, perhaps, Lord, if I were more than I am ... *(Quitely, sadly)* O God, I am like all the Hebrew people that have gone before me.

I have seen you. I have known your power even as the children of Israel saw their deliverance from Pharaoh's Egypt, your parting of the Red Sea for their exodus ... yet, like them, I too fear, I doubt, and I am ashamed of my own disbelief. So ... show me again ... a sign. *(GIDEON suddenly gets an idea.)*

Tonight, I will place a sheep's fleece on the

threshing floor and if there is dew only on the fleece and the ground is dry, then I will know that you will save Israel by my hand, as you said.

ANGEL OF THE LORD: *(Unseen but heard.)* **O Gideon, when will you trust?** *(GIDEON pantomimes picking up a fleece, and slowly, meaningfully, and with awe, he wrings water from the fleece.)*

GIDEON: *(A deep realization of the truth of the event.)* **God!** *(But again, a searching of his inner spirit)* **Lord, do not be angry with me, but let me make just one more request. Allow me one more test with the fleece. Then, I will really know you are with me. This time, overnight, make the fleece dry and the ground wet, covered with dew.**

ANGEL OF THE LORD: *(Unseen but heard.)* **And still, Gideon, you do not trust.** *(GIDEON pantomimes picking up a fleece, and slowly, meaningfully, and with even more awe he realizes the fleece is dry, the ground wet.)*

GIDEON: **The ground is . . . wet! The fleece is . . . dry!** *(Again realizing, but now a much deeper realization of the truth of the event)* **God!** *(An awe-filled face turns heavenward.)* **Your servant is ready.**

ANGEL OF THE LORD: **Gather together your soldiers.**
(From the audience, GIDEON selects fifteen-twenty youths and urges them to walk to the front of the staging area.)

ANGEL OF THE LORD: **Gideon, you have too many men for me to deliver Midian into your hands. In order that Israel may not boast against me that her own strength has saved her, announce now to the soldiers, "Anyone who trembles with fear may turn back and leave Mount Gilead."**
(GIDEON ad-libs the words of the ANGEL OF THE LORD, suggesting any "soldier who is afraid" may return to his place in the audience. Several youths do return to the audience.)

ANGEL OF THE LORD: **Gideon, there are yet too many men. Take them down to the brook, and there, I will select your soldiers.**
(GIDEON ad-libs the words of the ANGEL OF THE LORD, taking the remaining youths to an imaginary brook. He encourages the youths to "drink." GIDEON closely observes those who "drink.")

ANGEL OF THE LORD: Gideon, you still have too many men. Those soldiers that have not knelt down to drink, but kept their eyes searching the landscape — they will make the best soldiers. They shall be your army.

(GIDEON selects only three youths. These three did not bend their heads downward when getting a drink, but did indeed observe the surrounding landscape. GIDEON should endeavor to select those three youths who best satisfy this qualification for being a "soldier." The other soldiers are asked by GIDEON to return to their places in the audience.)

ANGEL OF THE LORD: Now, tonight I will give the Midianites into your hands.

(GIDEON now ad-libs the following pieces of stage business:)

1. *He selects several Midianites from the audience and has these individuals "camp" near the front of the staging area.*

2. *He instructs the three soldiers how to perform the task each will do during the night's "attack" on the Midianites (pantomimed).*

   — One soldier is encouraged to carry a lamp, let it drop to the ground, and make a loud "crashing" sound as he (or she) does this action.

   — The second soldier is encouraged to carry a trumpet and to blow this trumpet quite loudly during the attack. He encourages the soldier to practice blowing the trumpet.

   — The third soldier is encouraged to shout, "A sword for the Lord and for Gideon!" several times.

3. *When the three soldiers are sufficiently "rehearsed" and in their battle positions, GIDEON urges them to wait a moment as he then encourages the Midianites to "sleep" (pantomimed). He also instructs the Midianites to awaken quickly when they hear the noise of the Israelite soldiers and in their frenzy to "stab" themselves.*

4. *GIDEON then leads the Israelite soldiers into the Midianite camp, creeping into the camp, then on GIDEON's cue, smash lamps, blow trumpets, and shout, "A sword for the Lord and for Gideon!" The soldiers create much noise.*

> 5. *Startled out of their sleep, the Midianites do as previously instructed: awaking quickly, stabbing themselves in their frenzy, falling downward as if dead.*
> 6. *Proclaiming victory, GIDEON dismisses everyone involved within this brief scene and suggests they return to their places in the audience.*

ANGEL OF THE LORD: *(Unseen but heard.)* **I am the Lord your God, and this night, I have delivered the Midianites into your hands.**

GIDEON: **Thank you, God.** *(GIDEON moves to the center of the staging area, utilizing a psalm as praise.)* **I will sing to the Lord, for he is highly exalted.**

   I was but a youth, possessing only weakness; he made me strong, a mighty warrior.

(Now GIDEON and the ANGEL OF THE LORD speak antiphonally.)

GIDEON: **I will sing to the Lord,**

ANGEL OF THE LORD: **O Israel,**

GIDEON: **For he is highly exalted.**

ANGEL OF THE LORD: **I will make you into a great nation,**

GIDEON: **The Lord is my strength and my song;**

ANGEL OF THE LORD: **And I will bless you.**

GIDEON: **He has become my salvation.**

ANGEL OF THE LORD: **I will make your name great; and you will be a blessing.**

GIDEON: **He is my God, and I will praise him.**

ANGEL OF THE LORD: **I will bless those who bless you, and whoever curses you I will curse;**

(Now, GIDEON and the ANGEL OF THE LORD speak together.)

GIDEON: **The Lord will reign forever and ever. Sing to the Lord, for he is highly exalted.**

ANGEL OF THE LORD: **And all peoples on earth will be blessed through you.**

(Then the ANGEL OF THE LORD speaks alone.)

ANGEL OF THE LORD: **Do not be afraid, for I am your shield, and your very great reward.**

GIDEON: **Hear, O Israel, the Lord our God is one God.**

ANGEL OF THE LORD: **And you shall have no other gods before me.**

NABOTH'S VINEYARD
(I Kings 21)

Ahab, the king of Israel, envied his neighbor, Naboth's, expertise in growing grapes. Naboth was the hardworking farmer who owned the land adjacent to the king's royal household.

As he stared from his palace window watching both Naboth work and his grapes grow, Ahab's envy became an overpowering desire to own Naboth's vineyard.

Ahab visited Naboth, hoping to acquire the vineyard, but Naboth had no desire to deed over the vineyard. He said that it had been, and would continue to be, his family's inheritance.

Returning to his palace greatly disturbed, Ahab was confronted by his wife and queen, Jezebel, who declared her intentions to get for Ahab what he wanted!

And thus, Jezebel connived to have her way, using deceit, trickery, and prevarication. First she condemned Naboth as a "blasphemer," and subsequently had him put to death by stoning. Then, dead, the accused blasphemers property by Hebrew law became part of the royal household of Israel.

Ahab had gotten his vineyard!

Once again, the prophet Elijah was sent to pronounce judgment upon the feckless king.

Cast of Characters

AHAB
King of Israel
NABOTH
A hard-working farmer whose vineyard is his inheritance
JEZREEL
Adviser to the king
JEZEBEL
Wife to Ahab and queen of Israel

Note: The role of JEZREEL can be either male or female.

Scriptural background for this dramatization: *I Kings 21*.

Length of this dramatization: 30-40 minutes, depending upon the audience participation.

SCENE 1

AT RISE: JEZREEL, adviser to Israel's KING AHAB, enters the staging area, then walks to the front of the staging area, unrolls a scroll, and reads from the scroll as if reading from Holy Writ.

JEZREEL: **People of Israel, hear the Word of God as recorded in Holy Scripture:**
Naboth, a man from Jezreel, had a vineyard on the outskirts of the city near King Ahab's palace. One day, the king talked to Naboth about selling him this land. *(NABOTH enters the staging area at the mention of his name and pantomimes working in his vineyard. At the conclusion of the reading, JEZREEL exits the staging area as KING AHAB enters.)*

SCENE 2

AHAB: *(Shouting)* **Naboth! . . . Naboth!**
NABOTH: *(Stops his work momentarily.)* **Yes?**
AHAB: **I'm Ahab, King of Israel.**
NABOTH: **Yes, I know who you are.**
AHAB: **I have been admiring your vineyard.**
NABOTH: **Thank you. It is much work.**
AHAB: **Yes, I can believe that, and you obviously know well how to make the grapes grow!**
NABOTH: **I should. My family has been working this vineyard for a hundred years.**
AHAB: **A hundred years? On this hillside?**
NABOTH: **Yes, since David was king of Israel.**
AHAB: **Tell me, Naboth, do you make a good living tending this vineyard?**
NABOTH: **I feed my family.**
AHAB: **Yes, I'm glad you feed your family, but do you make a *good* living?**
NABOTH: **I get along . . . I'm satisfied.**
AHAB: **Ah, then, if you are merely *satisfied,* well, that means you could do better.**
NABOTH: **I guess everyone could do better.**
AHAB: **Naboth, I have been impressed with your vineyard, and now, I would like to make your**

vineyard part of my royal estate.

NABOTH: What?

AHAB: Your vineyard. I want your vineyard to become part of the royal household of Israel.

NABOTH: In other words, you want my vineyard for your own?

AHAB: You, Naboth, will become well-known! People all over Israel will know that you, Naboth, have been honored because of your hard work, your expertise and skill in growing grapes. You're truly privileged, Naboth, to have the king of Israel select your vineyard to become part of his own personal property.

NABOTH: Already, King Ahab, I am honored that you, the king of Israel, would even come to visit my humble field of grapes . . . and that is all the honor I need! I do not wish to become well-known.

AHAB: What man does not wish to become well-known?

NABOTH: Me.

AHAB: But you are foolish for not wanting —

NABOTH: I do not wish to become well-known at the expense of my family.

AHAB: Expense of your family? What foolishness! You understand me, Naboth, foolishness is that you do not realize this is an honor! I want to honor you, Naboth, throughout all of my kingdom.

NABOTH: Working land that has been in my family for a hundred years is honor enough for me, King Ahab.

AHAB: *(Snidely)* But you are poor, Naboth.

NABOTH: Most people in Israel are poor.

AHAB: Naboth, I want your vineyard!

NABOTH: I'm sorry, my king, but my vineyard is not —

AHAB: *(Trying a new tactic)* I'll buy it! I'll give you twice what it is worth!

NABOTH: You're generous, but —

AHAB: You'll become a wealthy man —

NABOTH: No, King Ahab, I won't become a wealthy man —

AHAB: Won't?

NABOTH: — because I'm not selling my vineyard!

AHAB: Not selling?

NABOTH: Yes, King Ahab, not selling!

AHAB: But I *am* the *king!*

NABOTH: And this *land* is *my* inheritance.

AHAB: I'll be back, Naboth. Maybe in time you'll change your mind.

NABOTH: My son expects this vineyard as his inheritance, King Ahab. I will not change my mind!

AHAB: *(Very disgruntled, he leaves the staging area.)* We shall see, Naboth, we shall see! *(AHAB exits the staging area, and NABOTH returns to his work.)*

SCENE 3

AT RISE: JEZREEL enters the staging area, again reading from the scroll.

JEZREEL: So Ahab went back to the palace angry and sullen. He refused to eat and went to bed with his face to the wall.

AHAB: *(Entering the staging area, shouting)* Jezreel! Jezreel!

JEZREEL: Yes?

AHAB: Where have you been all morning?

JEZREEL: I've been in the palace, working.

AHAB: Doing what?

JEZREEL: Counting money.

AHAB: Mine, I hope.

JEZREEL: Yours ... the annual grain harvest tax.

AHAB: And it was good?

JEZREEL: Better than ever.

AHAB: Good ... very good ... that means my army will be strong for yet another year ... and that means my enemies will continue to see and know my strength for yet another year!

JEZREEL: Yes.

AHAB: Israel is doing quite well these days —

JEZREEL: Since you have been king.

AHAB: Hah! I wish I could believe that!

JEZREEL: Don't you?

AHAB: No, I don't believe that ... because with all my strength and wealth, I can't get what I want!

JEZREEL: What is it that you want ... that you don't already have?

AHAB: Jezreel, look out that window! *(He points to the window.)* **What do you see?** *(JEZREEL walks toward the palace window being pointed out by AHAB. JEZREEL stares out this window.)* **Well . . . what do you see?**

JEZREEL: I'm not sure —

AHAB: Not sure? You fool! Keep looking!

JEZREEL: Ah, now I see.

AHAB: Yes?

JEZREEL: I see a hill.

AHAB: *(Losing patience with his adviser.)* **And what is on that hillside?**

JEZREEL: A man working —

AHAB: Yes, of course, it is a man working, but working where, in what?

JEZREEL: In a vineyard.

AHAB: A vineyard! Just *a vineyard* my adviser says . . . Well, look again.

JEZREEL: And what, my king, am I to see when I look again?

AHAB: You are to see the most beautiful vineyard ever!

JEZREEL: Oh.

AHAB: Now, tell me, isn't that vineyard the most beautiful you've ever seen?

JEZREEL: Yes, I guess.

AHAB: You guess?

JEZREEL: Well, your own vineyards are also beautiful.

AHAB: *Mine?* Nothing I have can even compare to the beauty of that hillside vineyard. Look at those strong branches and those thick clusters of huge, succulent grapes —

JEZREEL: Yours are equally as —

AHAB: I want that vineyard!

JEZREEL: Impossible!

AHAB: *Impossible?* For me, Ahab, king of Israel?

JEZREEL: Yes, even for you, Ahab, King of Israel.

AHAB: Why?

JEZREEL: That vineyard has been in Naboth's family for almost a century. It's an inheritance, handed down from father to son for five generations.

AHAB: So?

JEZREEL: So — Naboth is a poor man. He has nothing but that vineyard!

AHAB: All the more reason why I should have it. I can give him money, more money than he's ever seen . . . he'll be rich!

JEZREEL: Perhaps Naboth does not want to be rich.

AHAB: What man does not want to be rich?

JEZREEL: Naboth.

AHAB: *(Angered)* Naboth is a fool. He does not realize all that I am able to give him.

JEZREEL: Give or *take* from him?

AHAB: Take?

JEZREEL: Remember King David?

AHAB: What about King David?

JEZREEL: He also wanted a poor man's property: Bathsheba, the wife of Uriah the Hittite, a commander within his own army.

AHAB: *(Angrily)* Don't compare me to David!

JEZREEL: Why not?

AHAB: He made too many mistakes!

JEZREEL: Haven't you?

AHAB: What is this? You are supposed to be my counselor, my adviser, the keeper of my money. You do not tell me what to do as king!

JEZREEL: Ahab, you must not take Naboth's vineyard!

AHAB: *(Shouting)* Why not?

JEZREEL: Because that vineyard does not belong to you!

AHAB: *(Sniffs)* An old teaching.

JEZREEL: *(Correcting the king)* A commandment of God!

AHAB: Long since forgotten.

JEZREEL: Not by Israel's prophets —

AHAB: Today, kings take what they want!

JEZREEL: No!

AHAB: No? You can be easily replaced, Jezreel.

JEZREEL: Better to replace me because I speak the truth than to have blood on your hands —

AHAB: No? But I want Naboth's vineyard —

JEZREEL: It is not always wise to want another man's property.

AHAB: I order you to go to Naboth and get that vineyard.

JEZREEL: That is an order, King Ahab, I cannot fulfill.

AHAB: I have already been to see Naboth myself —

JEZREEL: And failed to convince Naboth that his

vineyard should be yours.

AHAB: Yes, but I will go again to Naboth. I will go again, and this time, this time, I will get what I want! I will get Naboth's vineyard. *(AHAB stomps out of the palace and re-enters NABOTH's vineyard.)*

SCENE 4

AHAB: Naboth, good morning to you.

NABOTH: Good morning again, King Ahab.

AHAB: Naboth, you work so hard, so very hard. I feel sorry for you.

NABOTH: Work is good, King Ahab, when done for a just cause.

AHAB: Ah, listen to the wisdom of this man! What you say is very wise, Naboth, very wise. And your hard work, Naboth, has been rewarded with a very fine vineyard.

NABOTH: You have already told me that this morning.

AHAB: So, I repeat myself. You will forgive me, Naboth, but I am getting old, and I am so very much impressed with your work and the results of your hard and most diligent work.

NABOTH: I am glad you are so impressed, my king, but again, I tell you I will not give or sell you my vineyard.

AHAB: Oh, is that why you think I've come?

NABOTH: Isn't it?

AHAB: No. I have come only to admire your vineyard.

NABOTH: Then admire.

AHAB: But I do wish such beauty could be preserved.

NABOTH: Such beauty has been preserved . . . through the work of my family.

AHAB: But that is much, much too limited. Your vineyard should be preserved for all Israel to see, to enjoy.

NABOTH: No.

AHAB: No?

NABOTH: No, my king, for when you say "for all the people of Israel to see and to enjoy," you really mean that you want my vineyard for your very own! No, King Ahab, my vineyard is my property and will be my son's property and his son's property. This vineyard is all that I have, all that I will ever have, and all that my sons will have.

AHAB: *(Furious)* We shall see, Naboth, we shall see! You cannot fly into the face of your king and hope to live —

NABOTH: My life is my land, and my land is my life.

AHAB: And I shall have them both.

NABOTH: No. No, you won't. *(AHAB angrily leaves the vineyard, moving toward the "palace" section of the staging area. NABOTH exits the staging area.)*

SCENE 5

AT RISE: JEZREEL enters the staging area, eyeing AHAB's return.

JEZREEL: You were not successful?

AHAB: No, I was not successful. Naboth continues to be so foolish —

JEZREEL: In whose eyes?

AHAB: He doesn't understand what this could mean to him . . . what I, the king, could give him: the honor, the privilege, wealth —

JEZREEL: Taking a man's only possession is not an honor nor a privilege.

AHAB: But I want Naboth's vineyard! *(JEZEBEL enters the rear of the staging area, quite indignant.)*

JEZEBEL: Ahab, you act like a child!

AHAB: Jezebel!

JEZEBEL: For two weeks I've heard you pouting and complaining about this vineyard.

AHAB: But just look out this window, and tell me if this isn't the most beautiful vineyard you have ever seen in your life!

JEZEBEL: In your eyes only.

AHAB: Perhaps, but that's the only person who counts.

JEZEBEL: Again, in your eyes only.

AHAB: I want that vineyard. Wouldn't you?

JEZEBEL: What do I care about a field of grapes?

AHAB: What do you care about anything except yourself?

JEZEBEL: And I've done fairly well for myself . . . and so should you.

AHAB: How?

JEZEBEL: By asserting yourself.

AHAB: By asserting myself?

JEZEBEL: If you want Naboth's vineyard, take it!

AHAB: Take it?

JEZEBEL: You are the king, aren't you?

AHAB: Yes, but —

JEZEBEL: But what? Take what you want! Take what you deserve as king!

AHAB: Jezebel, I can't *take* Naboth's vineyard, even if I am king!

JEZEBEL: Why not? Why can't you take a hillside field of grapes?

AHAB: The people of Israel will become concerned.

JEZEBEL: *(Laughing)* The people of Israel won't care. Why should they care? They'd take Naboth's vineyard themselves if they could.

AHAB: Israel's prophets will care. Elijah.

JEZEBEL: Elijah! Ha!

AHAB: Elijah stopped the rain from falling for three years here in Israel because of your idols, Jezebel.

JEZEBEL: And we're still here. Where is Elijah now?

AHAB: Who knows?

JEZEBEL: Who cares?

AHAB: But don't you understand, Jezebel, the people and prophets of Israel will call me a thief if I simply take Naboth's vineyard. I cannot afford to anger the people or prophets of Israel.

JEZEBEL: So, Ahab, you want the vineyard?

AHAB: Most definitely.

JEZEBEL: And the only reason you do not have the vineyard now is you fear the people and prophets of Israel will become in your words — *concerned?*

AHAB: Yes.

JEZEBEL: Then, Ahab, truly what a child you are.

AHAB: Watch your tongue, woman!

JEZEBEL: So, suddenly I am supposed to fear a most weak king!

AHAB: I am not a *weak* king!

JEZEBEL: Well, if you can't express your powers as king —

AHAB: What do you mean *if I can't express my powers as king?*

JEZEBEL: Just what I said, Ahab — today, kings command, peasants obey!

AHAB: I have already tried to tell you, Jezebel, I just cannot command Naboth to give me his vineyard —

JEZEBEL: Why not?

AHAB: Well —

JEZEBEL: Why not?

AHAB: Well, because —

JEZEBEL: Why can't you command Naboth to give you his vineyard?

JEZREEL: That would be stealing.

JEZEBEL: Stealing?

AHAB: That's right, Jezebel. Commanding Naboth to give me his vineyard would be the same as stealing.

JEZEBEL: Ahab, you disgust me. Your covetous desire to have Naboth's vineyard is no different than my telling you to take it!

AHAB: All right, Jezebel, once again, as in the past, I will listen to you —

JEZEBEL: Wise move, my king. I will devise a plan to get Naboth's vineyard, but a plan that will never let Israel or its prophets call you a thief!

AHAB: Fine, Jezebel. If you've got a plan that will get me Naboth's vineyard without anyone calling me a thief, then do it, and do it quickly.

JEZEBEL: You will never be called a thief, Ahab, my husband.

AHAB: But how will you do this, Jezebel?

JEZEBEL: Are you really a king or merely a weak man masquerading as —

AHAB: I am not *weak!*

JEZEBEL: Then stand aside and let me handle this!

AHAB: You?

JEZEBEL: I am queen of Israel, am I not?

AHAB: Yes.

JEZEBEL: Then, as queen of Israel, I will take Naboth's vineyard and make it part of your royal estate, Ahab —

AHAB: You're going to *take* it?

JEZEBEL: — but I won't be stealing, and you won't be

called a thief, Ahab.

AHAB: *(Enjoying the moment)* **Oh, good — good —**

JEZREEL: Remember, Jezebel, the people and prophets of Israel must not see Ahab as a —

AHAB: Silence, Jezreel! Let Jezebel work her plan!

(AHAB and JEZREEL exit the staging area.)

SCENE 6

JEZEBEL now addresses the audience, instructing the "members of the town council" to come forward. Several individuals from the audience come forward and seat themselves in front of JEZEBEL.

JEZEBEL now "instructs" the members of the town council, telling them NABOTH has committed the worst of all crimes in Israel: blasphemy against the name of the Lord God Jehovah!

She then demands the members of the town council do as the law of Israel states and commands: death of the blasphemer by stoning!

The members of the town council loudly agree.

JEZEBEL orders the town council to go to NABOTH's vineyard, which they do.

NABOTH has entered the staging area, specifically the "vineyard" section, and the members of the town council under the urging and direction of JEZEBEL move to the vineyard area shouting their anger, accusing NABOTH of "blasphemy!"

JEZEBEL then directs the members of the town council to pick up imaginary stones and hurl them at NABOTH, which they do.

NABOTH slumps to the ground and is carried Offstage, again by order of JEZEBEL.

JEZEBEL then asks the members of the town council to return to their places in the audience.

From the rear of the staging area, JEZREEL enters, strongly challenging JEZEBEL.

JEZREEL: Jezebel! You should not be doing this!

JEZEBEL: Who are you to tell me, Jezebel, queen of Israel, what to do?

JEZREEL: You have lied about Naboth.

JEZEBEL: I have gotten a vineyard!

JEZREEL: Falsely. Israel's prophets —

JEZEBEL: Israel's prophets do not threaten me! *(Calling loudly)* Ahab! Ahab!

AHAB: *(From Offstage)* Yes, my queen?

JEZEBEL: Naboth's vineyard is yours!

AHAB: *(Entering the staging area)* Oh, thank you, my queen.

JEZREEL: It was wrongly gotten —

AHAB: Wrongly gotten?

JEZEBEL: Do not listen to this sniveling adviser —

AHAB: How was Naboth's vineyard wrongly gotten?

JEZREEL: She, your queen, used treachery and deceit to have Naboth stoned to death.

AHAB: Naboth? Stoned to death?

JEZEBEL: I merely followed the law of Israel.

AHAB: What law of Israel?

JEZEBEL: The law that states: those who blaspheme the name of the Lord God Jehovah shall be stoned to death ... and immediately upon the blasphemer's stoning, any and all of his property immediately becomes the property of the king!

AHAB: Oh, good, my vineyard! My vineyard!

JEZREEL: Blasphemy, Ahab!

AHAB: So?

JEZREEL: But, Ahab, Jezebel accused Naboth of blasphemy!

AHAB: So ... if my queen accused Naboth of blasphemy, then I'm certain Naboth was guilty.

JEZREEL: *What?*

AHAB: Wasn't he, my queen? *(JEZEBEL does not answer.)* Wasn't he, my queen? *(Still, JEZEBEL does not answer.)* Wasn't he, my queen? *(And still, JEZEBEL does not respond.)* I asked you a question, Jezebel. Was Naboth guilty of blasphemy?

JEZREEL: No, never —

AHAB: If Naboth didn't blaspheme the name of the Lord God Jehovah, Jezebel, then how are you able to apply this law?

JEZEBEL: Ahab, you continue to disgust me. The people of Israel believe Naboth blasphemed God. They are not calling you a thief, which as I recall was your only concern. So who cares how I got the vineyard? Go, Ahab, take possession of your precious hillside. It's yours!

JEZREEL: It was gotten through blood.

JEZEBEL: You have what you wanted, Ahab, so go possess it, and never question me again! *(JEZEBEL angrily exits the staging area.)*

JEZREEL: Ahab, what Jezebel has done will bring you great harm.

AHAB: Why? What Jezebel has done was not my doing!

JEZREEL: She is your wife!

AHAB: What Jezebel may have done was her own idea. I had nothing to do with it.

JEZREEL: You wanted the vineyard.

AHAB: Why shouldn't I?

JEZREEL: Thou shalt not covet thy neighbor's possessions, one of the Ten Commandments.

AHAB: I don't care about old laws.

JEZREEL: Unless the *old law* works to your advantage like the law that got you the vineyard.

AHAB: *(Shouting)* Out of my sight!

JEZREEL: Banish me, O king, but you cannot banish your conscience.

AHAB: *(Shouting)* I wanted a vineyard! I wanted a vineyard!

JEZREEL: And now you have it, and with it you will also have God's wrath.

AHAB: God's wrath? *(JEZEBEL suddenly enters from the rear of the staging area.)*

JEZEBEL: Ahab! Elijah is outside the palace gates demanding to speak to you!

AHAB: *(Stunned)* Elijah? The prophet?

JEZEBEL: Is there another?

AHAB: What does he want?

JEZEBEL: What does he always want?

AHAB: He wants to condemn me! But why? Why should Elijah condemn me? *(AHAB and JEZEBEL "freeze" in their respective positions Onstage. JEZREEL reads from the scroll.)*

JEZREEL: But the Lord said to Elijah, "Go to Samaria to meet King Ahab. He will be at Naboth's vineyard, taking possession of it. Give him this message from me: 'Isn't killing Naboth bad enough? Must you rob him, too? Because you have done this, dogs shall lick your blood outside the city just as they licked the blood of Naboth.' "

"So, my enemy has found me!" Ahab exclaimed to Elijah.

"Yes," Elijah answered. "The Lord is going to bring great harm to you and sweep you away for you have made him very angry and have led all of Israel into sin."

DANIEL IN THE LIONS' DEN
(Daniel 6)

Like 25,000 other Hebrew youths, Daniel was carried into captivity by King Nebuchadnezzar's Babylonian soldiers in April of 597 BC.

Selected by the Babylonian forces at the command of King Nebuchadnezzar as being among the most intelligent, strongest, healthiest, and most attractive Hebrew boys (ages eight-fourteen), Daniel was taken to Babylon to be made into a "Babylonian."

But once in Babylon, Daniel began to evince powers considered "wondrous" and "powerful" by his Babylonian captors: he could interpret dreams.

As he did so, his fame spread, and soon Daniel was brought to the palace to interpret Nebuchadnezzar's troubling dreams, which were considered to be signs and omens from the Babylonian gods.

Speaking from wisdom and insight given him by the Hebrew Lord God Jehovah, Daniel interpreted the king's dreams, explaining their hidden meanings, warning the mighty ruler of future danger.

Daniel's favor and stature within the royal court grew, and he quickly became a most trusted member of the king's government, so much so that when a new king, the Mede Darius, ascended to the throne, Daniel was given a governmental position second only to the king himself!

But jealousy among Darius' other advisers fueled a conspiracy; a plot was connived and contrived to get rid of Daniel — forever!

A plot that would challenge Daniel in the only area that the vicious conspirators could find even a hint of fault: Daniel's Hebrew religion.

A plot that would send Daniel to the lions' den, a favorite form of punishment at this time. The victim was thrown into a subterranean den containing several hundred snarling lions, unfed for three to five days! The result, of course, was quick and immediate death!

But Daniel's God had another plan! A means to prove his power, enhance Daniel's position within the empire, and end the jealousy of his conspirators — forever!

Cast of Characters

DANIEL
A president of the Medo-Persian Empire, second in power
and authority only to King Darius, a Hebrew
DARIUS
King of Media-Persia
SYRIACK
MELZAR
Advisers to the king and president of Media-Persia

Note: The roles of SYRIACK and MELZAR can be either
male or female.

Scriptural background for this dramatization: *The Book of
Daniel* with emphasis on *Daniel 6.*

Length of this dramatization: 30-40 minutes, depending upon
the audience participation.

SCENE 1

AT RISE: DANIEL enters the staging area, praying as he enters.

DANIEL: O God, I am in a strange land. The Medes and Persians here don't believe in you. Help me to show them your power and to remain strong in my faith. *(During DANIEL's prayer, KING DARIUS has entered the staging area, listens, then comments.)*

DARIUS: Praying again, Daniel? And to which god among the many gods do you pray?

DANIEL: The one true God.

DARIUS: The one true God?

DANIEL: The Lord God Jehovah.

DARIUS: Daniel, we Persians have many gods.

DANIEL: King Darius, you Persians have idols, gods you've made with your own hands.

DARIUS: What?

DANIEL: With all due respect, O King, your gods are nothing more than wood and stone with hands that are useless, feet that don't move, mouths and ears that don't talk or hear!

DARIUS: But Daniel, you cannot see your god, and I can see all of mine.

DANIEL: Yes, you can see your gods, who do nothing! I can't see my God, but my God does mighty wonders!

DARIUS: Mighty wonders? Such as?

DANIEL: Such as Moses . . . when the wicked Pharaoh of Egypt held all the Hebrew people slaves, and God called Moses to lead his people out of Egypt.

DARIUS: And how does that show your God's power?

DANIEL: How? Greatly! The Hebrew people, my people, were walking through the desert when the Pharaoh decided to chase after them and carry them back to Egypt as slaves. Suddenly, my people saw hundreds of Pharaoh's chariots and thousands of Pharaoh's soldiers coming toward them and in front of my people was the Red Sea!

DARIUS: The Red Sea! *(Laughs)* Then there was no means of escape for your people!

DANIEL: But God parted the waters of the Red Sea, and

my people, with Moses, walked through the Red Sea on dry land to safety.

DARIUS: And Pharaoh's soldiers?

DANIEL: After the very last Hebrew was across to safety, God closed the Red Sea, and the chariots and soldiers were never able to get to my people.

DARIUS: Yes, your God was quite powerful.

DANIEL: And once, here in Babylon.

DARIUS: Here in Babylon?

DANIEL: Yes, before you became king, Nebuchadnezzar was king of the Babylonian Empire. Three of my best friends — Shadrach, Meshach, and Abednego — refused to bow down to Nebuchadnezzar's golden statue.

Nebuchadnezzar thought he was a god, and he wanted Shadrach, Meshach, and Abednego to worship him. But Shadrach, Meshach, and Abednego said they could only worship the Lord God Jehovah, not a man or an idol. Nebuchadnezzar became furious and threw Shadrach, Meshach, and Abednego into a very hot fiery furnace.

DARIUS: And what happened?

DANIEL: Shadrach, Meshach, and Abednego stood in the furnace — unharmed.

DARIUS: Unharmed?

DANIEL: Not even a hair on their heads was burned.

DARIUS: But how could that be possible in a fiery hot furnace? No one has ever escaped.

DANIEL: The Lord God Jehovah sent an angel to protect Shadrach, Meshach, and Abednego, and they walked freely in the furnace and sang praises to God.

DARIUS: Truly, your God, whoever he is, is most powerful. I hope your God will help you to rule over the affairs of my empire because I am today making you the chief president of my empire. You will be second only to me in power and authority throughout all of my empire!

DANIEL: You honor me with so much authority.

DARIUS: Our empire is very large.

DANIEL: Yes, it stretches for thousands of miles in any direction the eye can see.

DARIUS: I have been thinking my empire is too large

for the most effective control by one man. Therefore, I am dividing the empire into one hundred twenty provinces. Each province will be like a separate state, and each province will have a governor ruling over it. That governor will be my personal representative.

DANIEL: That sounds as if it is a good idea.

DARIUS: And I shall place three presidents over the one hundred twenty governors. That will mean all governors are responsible to my three presidents. And, in turn, the three presidents shall be directly responsible to me as king. *(SYRIACK and MELZAR enter the staging area.)*

SYRIACK AND MELZAR: King Darius, live forever!

SYRIACK: May your glory never be diminished!

MELZAR: And your wisdom everlasting!

DARIUS: Leave me, Daniel, while I speak with my two advisers. *(DANIEL exits the staging area.)* Ah, Syriack, Melzar, you have long been among my most loyal and most trusted advisers.

SYRIACK: We are honored to be your advisers.

DARIUS: You have served me well.

MELZAR: Service to you has been a privilege for us.

DARIUS: Today I will reward you both. For your many years of faithful loyal service, my good and wise advisers, I am giving you new titles, new positions of responsibility, new thrones of power.

From this day forward, you shall be known as presidents within my empire. You will rule over one hundred twenty governors from every province within the empire. I shall have three presidents over all my governors. And you, Syriack, and you, Melzar, will be two of those three.

SYRIACK: Three presidents?

MELZAR: And we are two of them?

DARIUS: The third president shall be ruler over you both.

SYRIACK: And who, O King, is the third president?

DARIUS: A man whose judgments I respect. A man whose opinions are shaped by honesty. A man I greatly trust.

MELZAR: Certainly, for you, O King, to have so much

confidence in one man, then this man must be truly great. We, too, shall honor and obey this third president.

SYRIACH: But tell us, O great King, who is this man? We must know who we will honor and obey.

DARIUS: Daniel.

SYRIACK AND MELZAR: Daniel!

SYRIACK: But Daniel is not of our country!

MELZAR: Daniel is a Hebrew captive!

DARIUS: True, Daniel was a Hebrew captive, but Daniel was brought here to our empire by Nebuchadnezzar to be made into the finest of Babylonians.

SYRIACK: But can you trust Daniel?

MELZAR: In the past, Daniel was not a great ruler of your empire. Daniel might change now. He might turn against you. He might lead a revolt and overthrow you, O King Darius.

DARIUS: Nonsense! I trust Daniel completely, and so will both of you! You, Syriack, and you, Melzar, will be responsible directly to Daniel for all the affairs of the empire. Is that understood?

SYRIACK: Yes, O great King, our allegiance is yours. We will serve you forever!

DARIUS: *(As he exits the staging area)* See that your allegiance is also to Daniel.

SYRIACK AND MELZAR: Long live King Darius!

DARIUS: I leave you now to attend to affairs of state.

SYRIACK AND MELZAR: Long live King Darius!

MELZAR: This should never have happened.

SYRIACK: Daniel doesn't belong here!

MELZAR: Daniel is not one of us! Why should we be responsible to him?

SYRIACK: Daniel is over us because he has been so friendly with King Darius, too friendly if you ask me.

MELZAR: But Syriack, Daniel does have wisdom.

SYRIACK: Wisdom? What wisdom?

MELZAR: Well, he has at times been able to interpret dreams. Also, Daniel has been able to answer mysterious riddles and happenings.

SYRIACK: Such as?

MELZAR: You forget so soon?

SYRIACK: Don't weary me playing games! Tell me what mysterious happenings.

MELZAR: At Belshazzar's feast.

SYRIACK: So?

MELZAR: *(Pantomiming)* **When that hand suddenly appeared from nowhere in the air. Remember that hand just hanging in the air! Then that hand began to write strange words on the palace wall. Daniel was the only person in the entire empire who could tell Belshazzar what the weird writing and strange words meant.**

SYRIACK: A trick!

MELZAR: No one else was even able to offer a guess as to what the words meant, but Daniel could. Daniel read the complete message and told us what it meant. Daniel said it was a message from his God.

SYRIACK: Nonsense!

MELZAR: Nonsense? **The whole incident was too frightening to me to say it was** *nonsense!* **Daniel's God must be very powerful.**

SYRIACK: Nonsense I say again. And you worry about nonsense while Daniel rises in power! In power over us! Daniel's God, huh! Daniel makes all that stuff up so King Darius will think he has some special power.

MELZAR: Maybe Daniel —

SYRIACK: Melzar, do you want Daniel to rule over you?

MELZAR: No.

SYRIACK: Do you want to be Daniel's slave?

MELZAR: Definitely not!

SYRIACK: Then Melzar, you and I must get rid of Daniel — forever!

MELZAR: And how are we going to do that?

SYRIACK: **We are going to make King Darius think Daniel is trying to destroy his empire.** *(SYRIACK and MELZAR exit the staging area as DANIEL and DARIUS enter another section of the staging area, very much involved in conversation.)*

DARIUS: You really believe in this God of yours!

DANIEL: Yes.

DARIUS: Someday I should like to see his power.

SYRIACK: *(From Offstage)* **King Darius! King Darius!**

DARIUS: *(Responding)* **Yes, Syriack?**

SYRIACK: *(Enters the staging area carrying an official-looking scroll.)* **King Darius, live forever! We come with a royal decree!**

DARIUS: A royal decree?

MELZAR: A royal decree for you to sign.

DARIUS: A royal decree for me to sign?

SYRIACK: For you to command into law throughout all of our empire.

DARIUS: What kind of law?

SYRIACK: O great King, Melzar and myself called a very important meeting.

MELZAR: We had all of your governors, princes, counselors, and army generals present. Hundreds of your loyal followers.

DARIUS: And what was the purpose of this meeting?

SYRIACK: To affirm how truly great and wise you are. We wanted all the world to recognize your greatness!

MELZAR: In fact, O King, we made a firm decree that you should be worshiped.

DARIUS: Worshiped?

MELZAR: Like a god.

DANIEL: Surely there is a better way to honor King Darius, Syriack and Melzar.

MELZAR: Better way?

SYRIACK: King Darius deserves such an honor.

MELZAR: King Darius deserves such obedience from his subjects.

DANIEL: But to be worshiped? A man is no god.

MELZAR: Listen to him, King Darius.

SYRIACK: He is taking away the honor you deserve. Everyone agrees that whoever prays should pray to you and only to you.

DARIUS: Pray to me?

SYRIACK: All men should pray to you, King Darius. When someone has a petition or a request, they should bring that petition or request to you.

DANIEL: But I cannot pray to a man ... even if it is my friend King Darius.

MELZAR: And those who don't —

SYRIACK: And we hope no one is so foolish as not to recognize your greatness, your power, O Mighty King —

MELZAR: But those who do not pray to you should be thrown immediately into a den of hungry lions!

SYRIACK: As a sign to all the world that you, O great King Darius, are the most powerful king ever!

DARIUS: A den of hungry lions!

SYRIACK: A just punishment, O King, to those so foolish not to pray to you.

DARIUS: But do we have a den of hungry lions?

MELZAR: We shall indeed make certain you do.

MELZAR and SYRIACK move toward the audience, select "lions," encourage the lions to move onto the staging area and form a circle.

Then MELZAR and SYRIACK instruct the lions to roar loudly whenever they hear the word "lions."

MELZAR: Now, King Darius, *(Showing him the scroll)* here is the decree.

SYRIACK: You have but to sign this decree, O King, and it becomes law. And everyone in the empire will immediately recognize your power, your greatness, your wisdom.

DARIUS: Truly, you do honor me, Syriack and Melzar. I will sign this decree. I will make your decree law, but only for thirty days. Everyone for the next thirty days shall pray to me and only to me, and those who do not shall be thrown into the den of hungry lions. *(DARIUS places his seal upon the scroll.)*

SYRIACK AND MELZAR: *(Bowing)* Truly, King Darius, may you live forever!

DARIUS: I will take this decree to my messengers and have it sent throughout all the empire. *(Exits the staging area.)*

SYRIACK: Well, Daniel, are you going to obey the new law?

MELZAR: Are you going to pray to King Darius?

DANIEL: I have already told you. I cannot pray to a man.

SYRIACK: Then perhaps you can pray to the lions as they gobble you up! *(SYRIACK and MELZAR laugh heartily as DANIEL exits the staging area. SYRIACK moves toward the lions.)* Just wait, good lions, it won't be much longer!

MELZAR: Very soon, great lions, you won't be hungry much longer! Soon you'll be fed —

SYRIACK: With Daniel! *(Both SYRIACK and MELZAR*

laugh.)

MELZAR: But how can we be sure, Syriack?

SYRIACK: Sure of what?

MELZAR: Sure Daniel ends up here inside the lions' den?

SYRIACK: *(Laughs)* Of that you can be certain. Daniel will not follow King Darius' decree!

MELZAR: But it is now law!

SYRIACK: Yes, our decree is now Darius' law! And it was so very easy to get Darius to make our plan the law of the land.

MELZAR: Darius is so conceited. He really does want everyone to worship him!

SYRIACK: And he really does think he should be worshiped! Imagine that! And now that is exactly what Daniel won't do!

MELZAR: But Darius may not enforce the law. Remember Daniel is his best and most trusted friend.

SYRIACK: Darius will have to enforce the law. It is a law he himself made. Do you think the one hundred twenty governors will follow King Darius if he doesn't enforce this law? Even if it does catch Daniel?

MELZAR: You're right, Syriack.

SYRIACK: Naturally. Now, let's go and catch Daniel in the act of disobeying the king's law.

MELZAR: And how will we do that?

SYRIACK: We'll hide near his house and wait until Daniel prays.

MELZAR: Then he disobeys King Darius' law.

SYRIACK: Then we get King Darius angry.

MELZAR: Then Daniel ends up in the lions' den.

SYRIACK: Then Daniel ends up in the lions' stomachs you mean!

MELZAR: Hold on, lions, it won't be too long. Daniel is coming your way. *(Laughing)* So sharpen your teeth, good lions!

SCENE 3

AT RISE: DANIEL enters the staging area, begins praying. As he prays, SYRIACK and MELZAR creep into the staging area near where DANIEL is praying.

DANIEL: O Lord, even as the shepherd boy David prayed in the psalm, so I pray deliver me from evil men. Preserve me from their violence for they are plotting against me. These proud men have set a trap to catch me. O Jehovah, My Lord, my God, hear my prayer.

SYRIACK: Ah-hah! Do you hear, Melzar?

MELZAR: Yes.

SYRIACK: And what do you hear, Melzar?

MELZAR: I hear Daniel praying.

SYRIACK: No, Melzar, you hear Daniel disobeying King Darius' command, King Darius' new law! And I think the king should know someone is disobeying his new law.

MELZAR: I agree, Syriack. The king would want to know. Shouldn't we be the ones to tell him?

SYRIACK: After all, we are King Darius' presidents, are we not! We are responsible to see that King Darius' law is followed and obeyed by everyone.

MELZAR: And that includes Daniel.

DANIEL: Don't let these wicked men succeed. Don't let them prosper and be proud. Let their plots boomerang! Let them be destroyed by the very evil they have planned for me!

SYRIACK: *(Moving toward DANIEL)* So Daniel, you are disobeying the new law!

MELZAR: You'll see the lions for this disobedience!

SYRIACK: Wait till we take you to King Darius!

MELZAR: Won't he be surprised to learn you are really a traitor!

> *SYRIACK and MELZAR select several individuals from the audience to become SOLDIERS.*
>
> *Following the selection process, SYRIACK orders the SOLDIERS to grab DANIEL and take their prisoner to KING DARIUS' palace.*

SYRIACK AND MELZAR: *(Calling)* King Darius! King Darius!

SYRIACK: O great King Darius!

MELZAR: Live forever!

DARIUS: *(Entering the staging area)* Syriack, Melzar, what brings you to my throne room? And with Daniel?

SYRIACK: O great King, we have sad news.

MELZAR: Bad news.

DARIUS: Sad news? Bad news? What is it?

SYRIACK;   Daniel was disobeying your decree, your new law.

DARIUS: That's impossible. Daniel is my most trusted friend.

MELZAR: He may be your most trusted friend —

SYRIACK: But he is causing trouble by disobeying your majesty's command.

MELZAR: He is showing that he himself thinks he is better than you, O great one.

SYRIACK: He was praying to his God.

MELZAR: He was not praying to you.

DARIUS: Daniel?

DANIEL: I do not think I am better than you, O King. You are my friend, but I am not able to pray to a man.

MELZAR: He was standing in his room praying loudly to his God.

SYRIACK: He was standing near his window —

MELZAR: Which was open.

SYRIACK: Anyone could see him —

MELZAR: Hear him.

SYRIACK: — even as we did!

MELZAR: See him disobeying your law!

SYRIACK: Hear him disobeying your law!

DARIUS: *(Stunned)* Daniel!

SYRIACK: We came immediately to you, O great King. News of Daniel's disobedience must not spread throughout the empire.

MELZAR: We wouldn't want other people to follow Daniel's example.

SYRIACK: He might become too powerful and try to overthrow you —

MELZAR: Foolishly, of course!

SYRIACK: But if he disobeys your law, O great King, perhaps he himself wants to be king.

DANIEL: I do not wish to be king!

SYRIACK: Then why doesn't he obey your command, King Darius?

DARIUS: I believe you, Daniel.

SYRIACK: But he broke the law.

MELZAR: Your law.

SYRIACK: Such disobedience requires immediate action. You must not let disobedience spread throughout your empire, King Darius.

DANIEL: The Lord God Jehovah is the only true and living God, and it is to him that I pray.

SYRIACK: But you are to pray to King Darius!

DANIEL: Darius may be king, but Darius is no god!

MELZAR: You have disobeyed the law of the empire.

SYRIACK: Great King, you have no choice —

MELZAR: But to show Daniel —

SYRIACK: Your greatness, your power.

DARIUS: Is it true, Daniel, what my presidents are saying?

DANIEL: Yes, I have been praying.

SYRIACK: As an act of disobedience to King Darius.

DANIEL: Not disobedience to King Darius, but obedience to the Lord God Jehovah.

SYRIACK: You see . . . he is not even sorry.

DANIEL: I can pray to no man.

DARIUS: Not even to me, your friend?

DANIEL: Not even to you, my friend. I can pray only to the Lord God Jehovah.

SYRIACK: Then you break our law.

DANIEL: And I will continue to pray to the Lord God Jehovah.

SYRIACK: Then you will continue to break our law. You will continue to disobey our king.

MELZAR: He will start a rebellion!

SYRIACK: Overthrow our great king! O great Darius, throw Daniel to the lions!

MELZAR: Show the world your power.

DARIUS: Daniel, I have no choice. You, the chief of my presidents, must surely know the importance of obeying my laws. You must know what I must do. If I do not enforce this law, what law will I be able to enforce in the future?

DANIEL: God will protect me.

DARIUS: I wish that I did not have —

SYRIACK: *(Laughing)* His God will protect him!

MELZAR: We'll see. Those lions are hungry. They have been starved for several days. They're just waiting for wicked people who disobey our great king's laws.

SYRIACK: Your majesty, there is nothing you can do. You signed the decree into law, and a law of the Medes and Persians cannot be changed! You must throw Daniel into the den of lions.

DARIUS: *(Addressing the SOLDIERS)* Take Daniel to the den of lions and throw him in! *(SYRIACK and MELZAR encourage the SOLDIERS to take DANIEL to the lions' den.)* And, Daniel, may your God whom you worship continually, deliver you. *(DARIUS exits the staging area.)*

SYRIACK: This will teach you —

MELZAR: And all the world —

SYRIACK: Not to disobey a command of King Darius!

MELZAR: Foolish Daniel! Into the den of lions you go! *(MELZAR urges the SOLDIERS to throw DANIEL into the den of lions.)*

SYRIACK: We will never hear from you again, Daniel.

MELZAR: Have a great meal, lions!

As SYRIACK and MELZAR exit, SYRIACK selects an individual from the audience, explaining the strange event that followed. The individual is encouraged to enter the den, touch the mouths of the lions, and through this touch the angel shuts quite tightly the mouths of the lions. The lions try to roar, but are unable to do so.

MELZAR and SYRIACK exit the staging area.

DARIUS: *(Entering the staging area)* O Daniel, servant of the living God, is it possible? Can it be? Was your God, whom you worship continually, able to deliver you from the lions?

DANIEL: *(From inside the den)* King Darius! Live forever!

DARIUS: Daniel! Are you still alive!

DANIEL: Very much so, King Darius!

DARIUS: But Daniel, how is this possible?

DANIEL: The Lord God Jehovah sent an angel.

DARIUS: An angel?

DANIEL: To shut the mouths of the lions. They could not even open their mouths! They couldn't even touch me!

DARIUS: Daniel, I will let you out of the den. Soldiers, *(Addressing the SOLDIERS from the audience)* get Daniel out of the den. *(The SOLDIERS do so.)*

DARIUS: Daniel, your God . . . your God is truly most powerful. He has saved you from the mouths of the lions!

DANIEL: As he did for the Hebrew people from Pharaoh's soldiers at the Red Sea, and Shadrach, Meshach, and Abednego from Nebuchadnezzar's fiery hot furnace.

DARIUS: Truly, *(Kneeling)* your God, your Lord God Jehovah, is the most powerful of gods.

DANIEL: He is the only true and living God, King Darius, and surely you now know I am innocent of trying to cause disobedience and rebellion within your empire.

DARIUS: I believe you, Daniel. It is Syriack and Melzar, my two other presidents, who are causing trouble . . . who are trying to bring rebellion to our empire. Soldiers, find Syriack and Melzar! *(The SOLDIERS immediately search for SYRIACK and MELZAR, who have entered the staging area curious to know what has happened with DANIEL. Upon entering, they are "chased" by the SOLDIERS.)* Soldiers, throw Syriack and Melzar into the den of lions! *(The SOLDIERS do as commanded.)* I decree that everyone shall tremble and fear before the God of Daniel in every part of my kingdom and throughout all the empire. For Daniel's God is the living, unchanging God whose kingdom shall never be destroyed and whose power shall never end. He delivers his people, preserving them from harm. He does great miracles in heaven and earth. It is he who delivered Daniel from the power of the lions.

DANIEL: *(Looking heavenward)* Thank you, God.

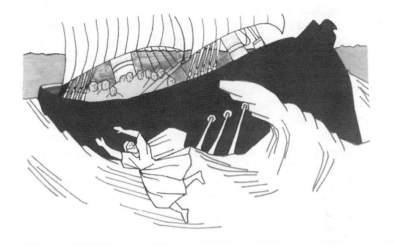

JONAH
(Jonah)

Jonah, whose Hebrew name means "dove," wanted very much to be a prophet, an individual utilized by the Lord God Jehovah to carry the Lord's message to the children of Israel.

To this end, Jonah worked, separating himself from his community. He spent many years in the study and meditation of the law and the prophets, the traditions, customs, and heritage of Judaism. He hoped the Lord God Jehovah would call him into service as a prophet to the Hebrew people.

From the tiny village of Gath-hepher near Nazareth, Jonah lived during the reign of Jeroboam II (ca. 786-746 BC). He had prophesied the restoration of a small section of Israel's borders. However, Jonah desired to be utilized by the Lord God Jehovah to a much greater extent and in a more meaningful way.

Suddenly and rather unexpectedly, Jonah found himself called by the Lord God Jehovah.

He was called not to Israel, but to his great chagrin to Nineveh!

Realizing Nineveh was the pagan capital of the large and extremely militaristic Assyrian Empire, Jonah became gravely concerned. He feared that his message would not be heard by those living within Nineveh. Or worse, he was certain his entrance into Nineveh would be his death.

He was faced with a moral dilemma: to obey the Lord God Jehovah and go to Nineveh, or forget his vow to serve the Lord God Jehovah as a prophet and not go to Nineveh. According to Scripture, Jonah decided to flee "from the presence of the Lord."

The story of Jonah, the prophet who first ran away from, then hurried to Nineveh to fulfill his mission, remains a challenging message to all desiring to serve, but are fearful to do so.

Cast of Characters

JONAH
A prophet of the Lord God Jehovah
NARRATOR
Who tells the story of the run-away prophet
JERESH
Friend to Jonah
SHIP CAPTAIN
The pilot of a ship heading toward Tarshish
KING OF NINEVEH
The ruler of the Assyrian capital

Note: This biblical dramatization can be performed by any combination of two to five actors.

If two actors are available, one actor creates the role of JONAH while the other actor plays the other roles, utilizing simple costume changes as a differentiation between characters.

If three actors are available, one actor creates the role of JONAH; another the NARRATOR and KING OF NINEVEH; the third JERESH and the SHIP CAPTAIN. Again, simple costume changes differentiate between characters.

If four actors are available, one actor creates the role of JONAH; the second actor creates the role of NARRATOR and KING OF NINEVEH; the third JERESH; and the fourth the SHIP CAPTAIN.

Scriptural background for this dramatization: *The Book of Jonah*.

Length of this dramatization: 35-40 minutes, depending upon audience participation.

SCENE 1

AT RISE: NARRATOR enters the staging area, walks to the front and speaks directly to the audience.

NARRATOR: Good evening. *(Appropriate greeting, depending on the time of the performance)* **The story we are about to tell you through drama is an important story concerning commitment and what commitment means or could mean.**

Ours is a true story that is in actuality a biography of a little-known figure, an individual who lived thousands of years ago, yet a character caught within the vice of a real-life situation that could happen to all of us with consequences that we could also feel and experience. *(Enter JONAH, walking toward the front of the staging area. NARRATOR describing JONAH.)* **At times, our subject was quite motivated.**

JONAH: Lord God Jehovah, I desire to be a prophet, your prophet. Lord, I want to stand on a hillside and bring your word to our people. I want to show our people, your chosen people, the right way to live, expressing your words, your feelings, your directives.

NARRATOR: — and our subject was quite earnest —

JONAH: I really want to be a prophet, Lord, and I'm willing, most willing, to go wherever you want me to go to speak to your people.

NARRATOR: — our subject was also quite prepared —

JONAH: And you will note, Lord, that I have been studying your word, reading and meditating on its deepest thoughts day and night.

NARRATOR: Truly, from all outward signs, from all intents and purposes, our subject was ready, willing, and able to be of service to his God ... at least until the actual moment of service came. *(The NARRATOR walks toward JONAH, stops, and addresses JONAH in a voice a bit more dignified than the voice he had been using when speaking as the Narrator.)* **Jonah —** *(JONAH looks around, trying to see who might be calling his name. He says nothing.)* **Jonah —**

JONAH: *(A bit fearful.)* **Yes? Who is it . . . that speaks to me . . . that I cannot see?** *(Then JONAH suddenly realizes who it might be; his expression changes from bewilderment to total surprise mingled with amazement.)* **God . . . is it you . . . really?** *(He kneels in respect.)*

NARRATOR: **Go to the great city of Nineveh —**

JONAH: **Nineveh? . . . Yes? . . . What about Nineveh?**

NARRATOR: **— and preach against it —**

JONAH: *(Rather meekly)* **Preach against it? But why?**

NARRATOR: **— because its wickedness has come up before me.** *(Almost immediately following the delivery of this message, the NARRATOR exits the staging area, leaving JONAH alone, worried, frightened, and probably a bit frustrated. JONAH remains kneeling, repeating to himself the message of the Lord God Jehovah.)*

JONAH: **Go to the great city of Nineveh and preach against it, because its wickedness has come up before me . . . Go to the great city of Nineveh . . .** *(Suddenly, JONAH realizes what he is repeating to himself. He stands straight up, as if struck by a bolt of lightning or perhaps more correctly, fear.)* **Nineveh! Nineveh! There's got to be some kind of mistake! Nineveh isn't in Israel . . . Nineveh's Assyrian, not Hebrew . . . why would I be sent to Nineveh? As a prophet? The Assyrians don't even acknowledge the Lord God Jehovah . . . they're pagan, evil . . . often our enemy. Why go there?** *(JONAH falls silent for a few moments as if pondering the reasoning behind the divine commandment. Then, certain there's been a misunderstanding, JONAH questions his God.)*

 God? Did I hear you right? Nineveh? *(JONAH pauses, hoping to receive an answer to his question. Hearing none, JONAH begins to "reason" with God.)*

 But Lord, Nineveh! Do you know anything about the place? *(Then realizes what a foolish question this was.)* **Oh, but of course, you do . . .** *(Then quickly, almost too quickly, as if covering up his inner fear)* **but let me remind you . . . Nineveh is the capital of Assyria . . . which is a very large empire . . . why compared to us, little tiny Israel, we're like a small mustard seed lying beside a giant oak!**

 Do you know the walls built around Nineveh

for its protection are so thick ... oh, but of course, you do, but let me remind you ... those walls are so thick that at any one point on the top of those walls, four chariots can have a race side by side!

And there are fifteen-hundred towers on the top of those walls ... each tower manned by spear-carrying soldiers just looking, waiting for an excuse to haul off and thrust that heavy iron spear into an intruder ... which is what I would be ... especially with such a message aimed right at their lifestyle!

Why would they listen to me? Oh, they might ... for a minute ... just long enough for me to tell them why I've come ... on a mission from the Hebrew Lord God Jehovah ... and then ... wham! *(Pantomimes feeling a spear thrust into his chest.)* **Right through the heart!**

Surely ... surely ... surely ... I heard you wrong ... let's see ... what other towns in Israel sound like Nineveh? Jerusalem, no way ... Could he have meant Hebron? No, doesn't sound anything like Nineveh. Shechem, Beersheba, Dan ... no, no town in Judea or Israel sounds like Nineveh. *(He pauses to think, to reflect.)* But a prophet to Nineveh?

I don't think Nineveh even knows what a Prophet is ... and, now, all of a sudden, they're going to have one! And one that's telling them there's trouble in Nineveh! Oh, there's going to be trouble for me in Nineveh!

Most of the time, Israel doesn't welcome its own prophets ... and Israel knows what prophets are! *(JERESH, a friend of JONAH's, enters the staging area.)*

JERESH: *(Enters in time to hear JONAH's last statement.)* **Don't be too certain.**

JONAH: *(Startled. Turns around to see his friend.)* **Of what?**

JERESH: **That Israel knows what prophets are. I overheard you talking to yourself.**

JONAH: **I wasn't exactly talking to myself.**

JERESH: *(Thinking there's something strange going on here)* **Oh, I see ... finally ...** *(Makes a downward nose diving gesture with his hand.)*

JONAH: **Jeresh, please ... I'm in a serious bind here ... we're talking pretty serious ...**

JERESH: Like how serious?

JONAH: Like I have something I'm to do for our Lord —

JERESH: That's serious.

JONAH: But it's not what I —

JERESH: — thought it would be?

JONAH: Ah ... yes and no. I mean, yes, because I've wanted to be a prophet, but no, I didn't expect to be sent as a prophet to where I'm being sent.

JERESH: Oh, you're being sent to a really bad part of town, huh?

JONAH: In a manner of speaking.

JERESH: Don't —

JONAH: Don't —

JERESH: Don't go. If it threatens life or limb, don't go.

JONAH: Well, it could definitely threaten life or limb, so to speak. My life and limb.

JERESH: Really? That serious? Here in Israel?

JONAH: That's just it. I'm not going to be a prophet in Israel. The Lord wants me to be a prophet to Nineveh!

JERESH: I suddenly see your concern.

JONAH: What am I going to do?

JERESH: What do you mean, what are you going to do?

JONAH: Just what I said, what am I going to do?

JERESH: There's only one thing you can do. Go.

JONAH: But a moment ago, you said *don't!*

JERESH: Well, that was before I realized who told you to go.

JONAH: I know. How can I refuse God —

JERESH: Well, many people do from time to time —

JONAH: But I have prayed to be a prophet ... over and over again ... I've studied and prepared myself to be a prophet ... for a long time ... and I want to be a prophet ... just not to Nineveh ... I mean it's difficult enough to be a prophet to Israel ... knowing you're going to be rejected from the moment you open your mouth ... but this way, being a prophet to Nineveh, you know you're not only going to be rejected, but like this will be the final rejection ... a **spear.** (*Again pantomimes a spear being thrust through his heart.*)

JERESH: Oh, Jonah, maybe it won't be so bad —

JONAH: But probably it will. The Assyrians don't even know about Jehovah.

JERESH: Then what a beautiful opportunity to tell them.

JONAH: As I'm dying?

JERESH: Surely the Lord God Jehovah wouldn't send you to Nineveh to — *(Can't quite bring himself to say the word "die.")*

JONAH: But it could happen.

JERESH: Jonah, when God sent Moses to speak to Pharaoh, I'm certain Moses must have felt the very same way you do. I mean there's not too much difference between the Pharaoh of Egypt and the King of Nineveh.

JONAH: Jeresh, I know our history. I understand the examples of faith and courage of our forefathers, but now that it's me ... knowing and understanding in my head doesn't seem to be knowing and understanding in my heart —

JERESH: Where's your faith, Jonah?

JONAH: It's not faith, it's practicality ... and the practicality of the situation is: Nineveh doesn't want me to enter its gates as a prophet.

JERESH: But God does!

JONAH: I know.

JERESH: *(Preparing to exit)* Then go to Nineveh, Jonah, and cry against it.

JONAH: *(Watching JERESH exit.)* Perhaps ... I should ... *(When JERESH has exited the staging area)* but I don't know if I can. *(JONAH hurries to another area within the total staging area. Without saying a word, he pantomimes preparing to leave. Then he does so.)*

SCENE 2

AT RISE: JONAH is wandering through the staging area, as if not exactly certain where he is going. Moments later, he sees an INDIVIDUAL standing near the front of the staging area. The INDIVIDUAL appears to be very much in charge of something. JONAH heads toward this INDIVIDUAL.

JONAH: Ah, sir? Sir? *(The INDIVIDUAL answers with a*

sort of grunt or perhaps a snort, nevertheless some kind of unexplainable interjection.) **Going somewhere, sir?**

CAPTAIN: Of course, that's my trade, going somewhere.

JONAH: Far . . . from here?

CAPTAIN: What's it to you?

JONAH: I've been thinking about going along.

CAPTAIN: Don't need any more men to work this ship.

JONAH: Oh, I wasn't thinking of working on board, I was thinking of booking passage —

CAPTAIN: We're strictly cargo.

JONAH: Even cargo ships sometimes carry passengers.

CAPTAIN: This isn't one of those times.

JONAH: Perhaps not, but where're you headed?

CAPTAIN: Persistent, aren't you?

JONAH: I need to get away for awhile —

CAPTAIN: In trouble?

JONAH: No, not the kind you're thinking of —

CAPTAIN: I've got enough problems of my own sailing the Great Sea without taking on board another problem.

JONAH: The Great Sea? You're sailing the Great Sea? To the west then?

CAPTAIN: To Tarshish, if you must know.

JONAH: Tarshish to the west . . . *(Then, to himself)* **quite a distance away from Nineveh to the east —**

CAPTAIN: What's that you say?

JONAH: I said, I'll pay you a good fare to take me west.

CAPTAIN: It could be a rough trip.

JONAH: But *(Pantomiming reaching into a bag of sorts to get some money)* **safer than where I was going.** *(Hands the CAPTAIN some money.)*

CAPTAIN: Get on board. Ship's leaving within the hour. I'll show you where you can stow your things. It's not much, but then again, a cargo slaver isn't meant to be much. *(JONAH gets "on board," following the CAPTAIN to another area of the staging area, which is actually another area of the "boat.")*

SCENE 3

The CAPTAIN now selects individuals from the audience whom he makes SAILORS on board his ship.

Actually, the SAILORS are slaves chained to the hold of the ship.

The CAPTAIN arranges the SAILOR-SLAVES in rows of three on the hold of the ship, then selects another individual from the audience.

This individual stands in front of the SAILOR-SLAVES and is instructed by the CAPTAIN to beat a drum. As the DRUMMER's right hand beats the drum (he also makes a banging sound as he beats the drum), the SAILOR-SLAVES pull their imaginary oars forward.

As the DRUMMER's left hand beats the drum, the SAILOR-SLAVES pull backward on their imaginary oars.

The CAPTAIN gets the ship "moving."

JONAH: I know. I'm not heading toward Nineveh, but what could I do? If I stayed home, if I remained home, I'd ever be reminded of — *(He doesn't complete this thought, but rather sits down in his cabin area as if feeling he's somehow failed.)*

CAPTAIN: Men, begin rowing!

JONAH: *(Standing up, pacing back and forth)* And if I'd gone to Nineveh, I'd be — well, I wouldn't be. I'd never be a prophet . . . I'm certain of that — because the soldiers on the walls would never even let me say why I was there.

CAPTAIN: Push off — into the open sea.

JONAH: A prophet's not to go beyond Israel . . . no prophet has ever gone beyond Israel's borders. A prophet is supposed to speak for God, directly to his people, carrying his message. How can I carry Jehovah's message to a pagan people, a people who don't even acknowledge Jehovah? *(JONAH sits down, depressed; then he looks heavenward.)*

Lord God Jehovah, I said I wanted to serve you, but I thought that service would take me among my own people. I never expected to be called beyond our borders to a non-believing people . . . This is too difficult for me . . . forgive my weakness.

The CAPTAIN then selects more individuals from the audience, placing them behind the "boat." Several individuals are instructed to create great peals of thunder. Others are asked to create lightning; others to sound as if rain falling and winds blowing.

The CAPTAIN thus orders into existence a "storm!"

CAPTAIN: Storm off starboard! Row harder, men! Row harder! Storm's getting worse! We'll all perish! We'll all drown! Lighten the ship, men! Throw cargo overboard! Row harder!

Why has this storm befallen us? Why should we all perish? Someone has caused this storm! Yes, this storm's someone's fault! *(Thinks a moment, then concludes)* Our passenger ... that wanderer ... I knew he meant trouble ... and that's who has brought this calamity upon us. *(The CAPTAIN moves toward JONAH's cabin and knocks on JONAH's door, arousing him. The CAPTAIN shouts.)* Hey, you ... you in there! We're all about to perish! We're all about to drown! *(JONAH pantomimes opening his cabin door, then looks directly at the CAPTAIN.)* Who are you?

JONAH: Jonah ben Amittai.

CAPTAIN: Why are you here?

JONAH: To escape a responsibility.

CAPTAIN: What?

JONAH: I'm on board your ship to avoid —

CAPTAIN: Look, the storm's getting worse! Why? Why are you on my ship?

JONAH: I am a Hebrew, and I worship the God who made not only the sea but also the dry land —

CAPTAIN: I don't care who you are. Just tell me, why have you brought this disaster upon us? We're all going to perish in the sea!

JONAH: I have been trying to tell you who I am —

CAPTAIN: I don't mean your name, Jonah ben Amittai, I mean *who* are you that would cause such a storm in this sea?

JONAH: I'm being reminded —

CAPTAIN: Reminded? Of what?

JONAH: Of what I didn't do, what I said I would do.

CAPTAIN: Look, Jonah ben Amittai, I don't know who you are, and I don't know what you're talking about, but I do know we're all about to perish if something isn't done fast, soon!

JONAH: *(Rather calmly, he states)* Throw me overboard.

CAPTAIN: What?

JONAH: Throw me overboard.

CAPTAIN: You'll drown within seconds of hitting the water.

JONAH: Then I'll drown, but this storm has come upon you because of me, and thus, getting rid of me will also calm down the sea, saving you and your men from perishing.

CAPTAIN: No, I can't throw you overboard. It's inhumane.

JONAH: It may be the only way to save yourselves.

CAPTAIN: No! We shall try other measures! *(The CAPTAIN leaves JONAH's cabin area and returns to the front of the ship, shouting as he walks.)* Throw more cargo overboard! You must lighten the ship, men, so our ship rides above these waves!

JONAH: *(Even as the CAPTAIN is shouting his orders)* Lord God Jehovah, you have found me ... Of course, I knew I couldn't run from you ... that indeed, I could only run from myself ... how foolish ... to think that running from myself, neglecting what I felt I was to do for you, would change my situation!

CAPTAIN: Throw more cargo overboard, men! Sailors, row harder! The storm's getting worse! We're going to drown! The ship's going to sink! *(The CAPTAIN moves quickly to JONAH's cabin.)*

JONAH: Throw me overboard, Captain.

CAPTAIN: But you'll perish!

JONAH: Then I perish.

CAPTAIN: *(Giving an order)* Men, throw Jonah ben Amittai overboard ... *(Looking heavenward)* and, God, do not hold me responsible for taking this man's life! *(In that instant, the CAPTAIN directs two SAILOR-SLAVES to throw JONAH overboard the ship.)*

    The CAPTAIN then describes the great fish that swallowed JONAH by selecting two more individuals from the audience, having them link hands, forming a circle, and encompassing JONAH.

    The CAPTAIN then notices the calming within the sea, the ending of the storm.

CAPTAIN: The storm ... it's dying down! We're spared! Men, row on!

    The CAPTAIN moves on, then out of the staging area, as if the ship also is leaving the staging area. The CAPTAIN

*also dismisses all those from the audience, asking them to
return to their places in the audience.*

SCENE 4

AT RISE: Inside the great "fish," JONAH sits forlornly,
penitently.

JONAH: *(Experiencing anguish; praying fervently.)* **Lord
God Jehovah, in my distress, from this watery grave
beneath the raging, swirling sea, I call out to you.
Hear my plea for forgiveness. And, Lord God
Jehovah, even as I am dying ... hear my pleas for
life ... and Lord God Jehovah ... should I survive
this great trouble in which I find myself ... because
of myself ... I tell you, my Creator, I will keep my
vow ... I will be your prophet. I will go where you
want me to go. I will say the words you want me to
say.**

     *Suddenly, following his prayer, JONAH finds
himself thrown out of the "fish's" stomach onto dry land.
The individuals from the audience who created the great
"fish" return to their places in the audience.*

JONAH: **Lord, what's happening?** *(Looking around
himself)* **I'm ... I'm ... on dry land! I'm not inside the
fish any longer! I'm spared ...** *(Kneeling)* **Oh, Lord
God Jehovah, thank you ... for my life.** *(From
Offstage, the NARRATOR once again becomes the voice of
God.)*

NARRATOR: **Go, Jonah, to the great city of Nineveh
and proclaim to it the message I gave you.**

JONAH: **Yes, Lord! I will, Lord! Thank you, Lord!**
*(JONAH hurries toward "Nineveh." Upon reaching
Nineveh, JONAH stands and looks at the might of the city.)*
**Look at those thick walls and those towers ... and
those soldiers looking at me ...** *(He repeats himself,
feeling his heart)* **looking at me ... is it my imagination
or are they pointing their spears in my direction?**

     **I remember Moses, Gideon ... I remember my
vow ...** *(He begins to walk toward the front of the staging
area as if walking inside the "city walls" and "gates." He
turns toward the audience as if about to shout to the people*

of Nineveh, which indeed, he does.) **People of Nineveh ... I bring a message from the Lord God Jehovah ...** *(He searches the top of the city walls for the soldiers, whom he believes are about to end his life with their spears.)* **Your wickedness has come up before the Lord God Jehovah ... and he, my God, wants you to know that unless you change your wicked ways within forty days ... Nineveh will be completely destroyed.** *(Even as JONAH is making such statements to the "people" of Nineveh, the KING OF NINEVEH is entering the front of the staging area, also in front of JONAH. He looks at JONAH.)*

KING: *(To his guards)* **Who is this man who threatens us?** *(Receiving no immediate answer, he looks about the room, then upward, snorting.)* **Ehh?** *(Still silence.)* **Bring him to me!**

JONAH: **I warn you, Nineveh, decide now: forty days to change your wicked ways or destruction will fell your thick walls and drop your soldiers as if your warriors were mere flies being swept away by a great wind and your walls, your security, crumbling as if a field of grain being scythed by a harvester.** *(The KING moves closer to JONAH.)*

KING: **Who are you, little man, that you should threaten us?**

JONAH: **A messenger —**

KING: **Obviously —**

JONAH: **— from the Lord God Jehovah.**

KING: **The Lord God Jehovah?** *(With cynicism)* **Really.** *(With a definiteness in his tone)* **I know no Lord God Jehovah.**

JONAH: **He is the God of the Hebrews.**

KING: **Then why does he come here, little messenger?**

JONAH: **Because Jehovah is more than the God of the Hebrews —**

KING: *(Again, a bit cynical.)* **Really?**

JONAH: **Jehovah is the creator of the universe —**

KING: **Even Nineveh?**

JONAH: **Even Nineveh.**

KING: **Which he now threatens with destruction.**

JONAH: **No. Jehovah does not threaten destruction. You carry your own destruction.**

KING: **Our own destruction?**

JONAH: Through your wickedness. Your moral decay, your forsaking of your own principles of decency, your treating of honesty as if that quality was foreign to you ... these wicked habits, this evil lifestyle ... this is what threatens to bring about your own destruction.

KING: I see. *(Trying to utilize logic)* Tell me, little man —

JONAH: *(Correcting the king)* Jonah ben Amittai.

KING: *(Accepting the correction, he repeats the name with a slight cynical bow and tone within his voice.)* Jonah ben Amittai ... have you been in Nineveh before this sudden entrance within my city gates?

JONAH: No.

KING: Then certainly, for a stranger to my land, you have quite definite opinions about how we live. How can you know how we live if your first entrance into my city is today, the same day you pronounce destruction upon us?

JONAH: A man does not need to enter a city to know of its wickedness. Such news travels faster than an eagle soaring on a great wind's current.

KING: And your God sends you here?

JONAH: Yes.

KING: Why?

JONAH: Why?

KING: Yes, why would your God send you here to us in Nineveh? Perhaps this is some fiendish plot by the people of Israel —

JONAH: Oh, king, truly you have more wisdom than that ... certainly, your own spies would tell you that Israel is far too weak to threaten the existence of Nineveh, indeed the entire Assyrian Empire. No, O king, I come not as a conspirator wishing you ill ... though I could wish your country ill because of its evil ... I come only as a servant of my God —

KING: A servant? Jonah ben Amittai, you cause me great concern. You enter my city and begin shouting unannounced —

JONAH: I walked for an entire day within your city before I began proclaiming God's message. Surely, within that day, your soldiers brought word to you of my presence in Nineveh.

KING: Of course, but we let you live because we were surprised to see a lone Hebrew traveling within enemy territory so to speak ... alone and unarmed —

JONAH: It was not easy, O king —

KING: Of course ... so since you came into our midst alone and unarmed, I can only presume there are others waiting to follow you ... waiting for a signal from you to wage war —

JONAH: Have you seen signs of an approaching army? Have your caravans returning from trade with Egypt told you of armies marching this way? No, O king, you have been told of no such armies, no such threats, just merely one lone prophet making his way through the desert to speak with you ... before one who is greater than any army wrecks damage upon you.

KING: This one who is greater than any army ... this is the God you speak of ... this Jehovah —

JONAH: Yes.

KING: You would risk your life to save ours?

JONAH: Yes ... because my God sent me.

KING: Why? Why would a foreign God care to save us?

JONAH: Because you are people, his creation. *(The KING ponders all that he has heard, then, carefully makes a decision.)*

KING: I believe you, Jonah ben Amittai ... I believe you ... and your God. *(The KING "ascends" upward to his throne area, then turns and makes a proclamation.)* **By the decree of the king and his nobles:**

Do not let any man or beast, herd or flock, taste anything; do not let them eat or drink. But let man and beast be covered with sackcloth. Let everyone call urgently on God. Let them give up their evil ways and their violence. Who knows? God may yet relent and with compassion turn from his fierce anger so that we will not perish. *(During the above proclamation, JONAH exits the staging area.)*

Following the proclamation, the KING descends his throne area, and upon his descent, becomes once again the NARRATOR, who picks up a scroll and reads:

NARRATOR: *(Reading from a scroll as if reading from Scripture)* **"When God saw what they did and how** they turned from their evil ways, he had compassion and did not bring upon them the destruction he had threatened."

And what of Jonah, the subject of this brief drama? What did he learn?

Perhaps what we should all learn: that our God, the creator of the universe, is much larger, much greater than our own little worlds ... that our commitments to him and to ourselves demand more of ourselves than mere words ... and that a vow — spoken only — remains but noise until brought into action ... by you.

Section III

ONE-PERSON DRAMATIZATION

I, PAUL*
(Acts)

Creating a one-person dramatization can be a unique and satisfying dramatic experience.

I, Paul details the life, work, and ministry of the Apostle Paul, who first as the Pharisee Saul, plotted to destroy all believers in Jesus Christ. Following a blinding vision on the road to Damascus, he, himself, became an ardent follower of the Carpenter from Galilee. He then traveled throughout much of the then known world to share the good news of the Gospel of Jesus Christ.

Opening with Paul's trial in Rome where he defended his new religious faith, the play, *I, Paul*, then takes both the actor and the audience through much of the great missionary's life. From his anger against the followers of Jesus Christ as Saul, to his conversion as Paul, he led a life of

---

persecution, missionary service, teaching, preaching, and writing. Everything he did was in the name of his Lord Jesus Christ. He wanted to open to a broader community the claims of the resurrected Messiah.

To perform *I, Paul,* is to return to the first century AD when believers within the Lord Jesus Christ struggled to maintain their faith in a world eagerly seeking their demise. It is to experience the dynamic power of this little man proclaiming in a mighty way God's message!

The "changes" within Paul's character and personality from the persecutor, Saul, to the persecuted, Paul, can most easily be seen on stage with a simple addition of an outer garment or cloak to the standard first-century biblical costume.

AT RISE: The Apostle PAUL, looking old, haggard, the victim
of beatings, a stoning, and imprisonment, his hands bound
with chains, walks very slowly down the center aisle of
the staging area. At the front of the stage, he suddenly
turns toward his audience and powerfully addresses not
only his captors but also his accusers.

PAUL: I, Paul ... appeal to Caesar ... *(PAUL looks at
his bonds, then to his captors.)*
      Because of the hope of Israel ... I am now
bound ... with this chain.
      I do not have any charge to bring against my
own people ... but rather they against me.
      Although I have done nothing against our
people or against the customs of our ancestors, I
was arrested in Jerusalem and handed over to the
Romans.
      They examined me and wanted to release me
because I was not guilty of any crime deserving
death. But when the Jews objected, I myself was
compelled to appeal to Caesar. *(PAUL looks intently
at his audience, expressing the reason and purpose
supporting his current conversation with them.)*
      For this reason, my brothers, I have asked to
see you, to talk with you ... that you may know
Jesus Christ, our Messiah, our hope of glory, and
also, in part, that you may know more about
me ... formerly Saul, a Pharisee of the
Pharisees ... now, Paul, a servant and Apostle of
Jesus Christ, and most recently ... a
prisoner ... beaten, bound, shackled.
      Yet ... even though a prisoner because I spoke
boldly the truth about Jesus Christ, I am not
ashamed of the gospel because it is the power of
God for the salvation of everyone who believes: first
for the Jew ... then for the Gentile.
      For in the gospel a righteousness from God is
revealed, a righteousness that is by faith. To this
gospel, I affirm my loyalty, my devotion, my very
life. I pray that I will always have sufficient courage
so that now ... as always ... Christ will be exalted
in my body ... whether by life or by death. I have

known both. ... *(PAUL now brings years of experience, years of suffering to bear upon this moment, this recitation of endurance for the sake of the gospel.)*
... **for the defense of the gospel. I have been in prison frequently ... flogged most severely ... exposed to death again and again.**

Five times I was whipped with thirty-nine lashes, three times I was beaten with rods. Once, I was stoned. Three times I was shipwrecked. And once I spent a night and a day in the open sea.

I have been in danger from rivers, in danger from bandits, in danger from my own countrymen, from Gentiles, from false brothers. In danger in the city, in the country, at sea. I have labored and toiled and have often gone without sleep ... I have known hunger and thirst and have often gone without food ... I have been cold and naked. Truly, I can say: For me to live is Christ ... and to die is gain. *(PAUL unwraps the chains that bind his hands. Once unbound, he pulls on a cloak, and during the act of pulling on the cloak, he becomes young, vigorous, SAUL. Sincerity now fills his face, where moments earlier conflict and struggle were evidenced.)*

SAUL: *(In Jerusalem)* **I have not always felt so kindly or so strongly about the gospel of Jesus Christ. In fact, during most of my life, I regarded myself a "Hebrew of the Hebrews."**

As a youth, I was a diligent student of the law of Moses with the master teacher and Pharisee Gamaliel.

As a young man, I myself became a Pharisee. I taught in our synagogues with strictest authority to the minutest details of the law. I advocated its most stringent demands, ascetic limitations, and the rigid austerity that it imposed upon an individual. And I debated the law's every jot and tittle most persuasively with a finality that permitted little deviation.

I, Saul of Tarsus, was most zealous to keep our precious Judaism pure. I was even more determined to keep our Hebrew people, the true children of God, intent upon stern adherence to the law's most exact

interpretation. Any deviation from the law by anyone was infidelity to the Scriptures, tantamount to blasphemy of the most high God.

Thus, the words of Jesus, a "self-proclaimed" Messiah, were as blasphemy to me!

To claim that he was the fulfillment of the law and the prophets! To imply that he could forgive sins! To teach that he was equal to God, in fact that he himself was God!

Evil, malicious blasphemy! Blasphemy that demanded as the law states... *death!* But death... did not silence his voice! Foolish, misled followers of this crucified carpenter spoke for him!

Throughout Judea, these ill-advised peasants uttered his teachings, proclaimed his deity, lauded his actions.

These ignorant villagers were undermining the religious structure of Judaism. Their misguided allegiance to a dead man named Jesus was causing disputes and creating dissension among our people. Their praises were polluting our homes, our synagogues, our minds. Their fallacious exhortation that a man who spoke the name of the Lord God Jehovah and was put to death on a cross, still lives. This is blasphemy! He has not arisen from the dead!

I wanted this erroneous babble stopped!

To debate the law's many meanings in the synagogues was one thing, to defile our very lives with blasphemous teachings was quite another!

I wanted these villagers, who had become the dead carpenter's voice, his feet, his hands, to recant their allegiance to a supposedly risen Lord!

Risen Lord!

These fools were his resurrection!

I wanted them dead! Everyone of them. Dead... like their "carpenter-teacher."

And to see that this was accomplished, I opposed them in every possible way. I persecuted and tortured them... these followers of Christ. I gave assent to the stoning of Stephen, personally standing by, urging those hurling stones to do so without mercy!

Thus, my hatred of these false Messiah followers — fueled by my earnest desire to serve God by keeping the law pure — spirited me toward Damascus.

Many of his believers were there ... and in Damascus, I would begin a vengeful search. This would be authorized by the high priest himself. I would find, shackle, and imprison any and all followers of this dead Jesus!

I would rid the world of these misguided disciples of a dead carpenter's son!

Yet ... never once ... not even for a moment ... had I considered that this Jesus might truly have been more than a wandering Judean. Until ... on the road to Damascus ... *(The following narrative is re-enacted. Thus, SAUL pantomimes the events he is describing, literally reliving these events.)* A brilliant light from heaven encompassed me! Startled and frightened, I fell to the ground, covering my eyes, hiding from the radiance of this mysterious light! When suddenly, seemingly from within the light, a voice called to me ... "Saul ... Saul ..." I was stunned!

"Why do you persecute me?" Lying there prostrate in the dust on the road, I choked, "Who are you ... Lord?" But I knew ... even as I asked.

"I am Jesus ... whom you are persecuting ..."

In that instant, I knew I had been wrong, that I had tragically opposed truth, that Jesus whom I thought dead was alive!

I was humbled, broken. I clung to the ground, ashamed to look upward into the radiant face of my Lord.

Then Jesus spoke to me again, this time with an order:

"Get up, go into the city, and you will be told what you must do."

I will be told what I must do! What I must do? I repeated this statement over and over in my mind ... astounded, overwhelmed. What I must do?

The risen Lord appearing to me ... personally, from the heights of heaven, commissioning me ...

**me, the persecutor to do a task! For him! The Son
of God!**

Speechless, I struggled to my feet. *(As he
struggles to his feet, he reaches toward his eyes, not
completely comprehending his current physical situation.)*

Blind! I'm blind! *(He is saddened, lacking any will
of his own, completely subservient to a divine power.)* **O
Lord God Jehovah, I am your servant. Do with me
as you will.**

*(SAUL/PAUL stands up from his sprawled position
on the floor. From his natural appearance, it is evident
SAUL is blind.*

*(He extends his right hand outward . . . as if "feeling
his way" and walks toward Damascus. At first, he stumbles,
almost falls; then he picks himself up again and continues
to walk.*

*(This is a pathetic scene: a once vigorous young man,
a strong leader, reduced to a faltering, inadequate,
uncertain individual, who knows the hand of God has
touched him personally. He simultaneously feels frightened
and privileged.*

*(When he reaches his "destination," SAUL seats
himself, holding his bowed head between his hands, forlorn
and saddened by the recent turn of events. He is most
solemn.*

*(Slowly, deliberately, he looks upward, speaking
cautiously to someone who has entered the room. The
someone, ANANIAS, stands to his "left" and is, of course,
invisible to the audience.)*

SAUL: **Yes?**

I am he, Saul of Tarsus.

**You are a follower of Jesus with a message for
me? Come closer, Ananias. Tell me what the message is.**

**Please don't be afraid, I won't hurt you. I can't.
I'm blind.**

**Yes, I do believe. I do believe Jesus is our long-
awaited Messiah . . . and our . . . my Saviour. He
wants me to proclaim his death and resurrection
. . . his salvation to the people of Israel and before
the Gentiles and their kings?** *(SAUL now speaks with
a profound awareness of his own unworthiness.)*

Me? But I was the one who persecuted . . .

tortured . . . Even you, Ananias, were first afraid of me.
Yet, if this is what my Lord wants, then I am willing.
(SAUL looks upward. ANANIAS moves toward SAUL. ANANIAS stretches his hands forward to touch SAUL's blind eyes. SAUL reaches upward and grasps ANANIAS' wrists even as ANANIAS' fingers touch his eyes. Instantly, SAUL is able to see. He is overjoyed, but also awed.) I see! I can see! *(SAUL stands upright, a "changed" person. A total, complete conversion has occurred.)*

PAUL: I, Saul, will make Jesus known. I will proclaim his death, his resurrection, his salvation.

Me . . . once the persecutor, now the "sent one." Once the one who silenced his followers' voices . . . now the one who heralds his truths! Once driven by human hatred . . . now impelled by divine command!

Once the Pharisee of the Pharisees . . . now an Apostle of Jesus Christ.

Once Saul, now Paul!

(Now, a new creation born of the spirit, PAUL walks vigorously about the staging area, also throughout the audience, befitting his sermons. PAUL preaches.)

Men of Israel . . . and you God-fearing Gentiles . . . listen to me!

As he promised, the God of the people of Israel has brought to you the Saviour Jesus . . . and it is to us that this message of salvation has been sent.

But the people of Jerusalem and their rulers did not recognize Jesus, yet in condemning him they fulfilled the words of the prophets that are read every Sabbath.

Though they found no proper ground for a death sentence, they asked Pilate to have him executed. When they had carried out all that was written about him, they took him down from the tree and laid him in a tomb.

But God raised him from the dead, and for many days he was seen by those who had traveled with him from Galilee to Jerusalem. They are now his witnesses to our people.

We tell you the good news: what God promised

our fathers he has fulfilled for us, their children, by raising up Jesus. Therefore, my brothers, I want you to know that through Jesus the forgiveness of sins is proclaimed to you. *(PAUL pauses from his preaching. He sees someone who needs his help. He walks toward the man lame from birth. PAUL extends his hand downward.)*

I hear you, lame one, calling on the name of our Lord and Saviour Jesus Christ. Your faith in him has made you whole. Stand on your feet! *(PAUL watches the man stand to his feet and then walk.)*

You're healed! *(PAUL turns and stares upward and "into the distance." PAUL is having a vision.)*

God, what is it? Who is it? I see . . . I see a man. He looks as if he is from . . . Greece. Yes, he looks Greek . . . and . . . he's   talking.   No.   He's calling . . . begging me to come to Macedonia and help him. *(The vision ended, PAUL journeys toward "Greece." Seconds later, he preaches boldly.)*

Men of Athens! I see that in every way you are very religious. For as I walked around and observed your objects of worship, I even found an altar with this inscription: "To an uknown God."

Now what you worship as something unknown, I am going to proclaim to you.

The God who made the world and everything in it is the Lord of heaven and earth and does not live in temples built by hands. And he is not served by human hands, as if he needed anything, because he himself gives all men life and breath and everything else.

From one man he made every nation of men, that they should inhabit the whole earth. He determined the times set for them and the exact places where they should live. God did this so that men would seek him and perhaps reach out for him and find him. He is not far from each one of us.

"For in him we live and move and have our being." As some of your own poets have said, "We are his offspring."

Therefore, since we are God's offspring, we should not think that the divine being is like gold or silver or stone . . . an image made by man's design and skill. In the past, God overlooked such ignorance, but now he commands all people everywhere to repent.

For he has set a day when he will judge the world with justice by the man he has appointed. He has given proof of this to all men by raising him from the dead. *(PAUL notices a young girl possessed by a demon. He stops abruptly.)*

Spirit, why do you trouble that slave girl? You are driving her to do unholy, ungodly acts! In the name of Jesus Christ, I command you to come out of her! *(After the exorcism, PAUL rejoices.)* God, be praised! *(Then PAUL turns. He sees a young man lying dead on the ground. With great compassion, PAUL kneels beside the dead body.)*

Do not be frightened. Eutychus is not dead. He has merely fallen asleep.

Arise! Walk! Return to life!

He's alive!

Yet, even as I taught about our living Messiah ... his love, his death, his resurrection, his salvation ... and even with wondrous signs and miracles performed in his name ... many did not believe, even as I had not believed at first ...

Many created trouble, even as I had done ... Some wished me dead, even as I had done.

In Damascus, those who followed Jesus thought me a wolf in sheep's clothing, yet a mortal threat to their safety.

Those who upheld the Hebrew law thought me a traitor. They plotted to kill me. My assassins kept watch on the city gates day and night waiting for the opportunity to kill me. But I learned of the conspiracy and had myself lowered over the wall in a basket late at night.

I escaped to Jerusalem. Only to become a target for death ... because I spoke boldly the truth of Jesus Christ. And even as my enemies plotted, I escaped with the help of friends to Caesarea, then to Tarsus.

But condemnation and persecution increased. In Lystra, I was stoned. In Philippi, I was stripped, beaten, whipped, and thrown into prison.

Brothers, listen now to my defense. I am a Hebrew. Under Gamaliel, I was thoroughly trained in the law of our fathers and was just as zealous for God as any of you are today.

But now follow Jesus, our Messiah. *(The soldiers strike PAUL in the mouth.)*

You have struck me . . . but God will strike you. You sit there to judge me according to the law, yet you yourself violate the law by commanding that I be struck!

My brothers, I am a Pharisee, the son of a Pharisee. I stand on trial because of my hope in the resurrection of the dead.

But we know that in all things God works for the good of those who love him, who have been called according to his purpose.

What then shall we say in response to this?

If God is for us, who can be against us?

Who shall separate us from the love of Christ? Shall trouble or hardship or persecution or famine or nakedness or danger or sword?

No, in all these things we are more than conquerors through him who loved us. For I am convinced that neither death nor life, neither angels nor demons, neither present nor the future, nor any powers, neither height nor depth, nor anything else in all creation, will be able to separate us from the love of God that is in Christ Jesus our Lord. *(PAUL sits down, begins writing.)*

And what is love . . . If I speak in the tongues of men and of angels, but have not love, I am only a resounding gong or a clanging cymbal.

If I have the gift of prophecy and can fathom all mysteries and all knowledge, and if I have a faith that can move mountains, but have not love, I am nothing.

If I give all I possess to the poor and surrender my body to the flames, but have not love, I gain nothing.

Love is patient, love is kind. It does not envy, it does not boast, it is not proud. It is not rude, it is not self-seeking, it is not easily angered, it keeps no record of wrongs.

Love does not delight in evil but rejoices with the truth. It always protects, always trusts, always hopes, always perseveres.

Love never fails.

But where there are prophecies, they will cease; where there are tongues, they will be stilled; where there is knowledge, it will pass away.

And now these three remain: faith, hope, and love. But the greatest of these is love. *(PAUL now stands, looks quite tired, very weary.)*

I desire to depart this life and be with Christ, which is better by far ... but it is more necessary for you that I remain ... so that through my being with you ... again your joy in Christ Jesus will overflow.

Though I am free and belong to no man, I make myself a slave to everyone to win as many as possible. To the Hebrews, I became like a Hebrew to win the Hebrews.

To those under the law, I became like one under the law ... so as to win those under the law.

To those not having the law, I became like one not having the law ... so as to win those not having the law.

To the weak, I became weak, to win the weak. I have become all things to all men so that by all possible means I might save some. I do all this for the sake of the gospel ... to which I was called to be an Apostle ... and set apart for the gospel of God ... the gospel he promised beforehand through his prophets in the Holy Scriptures regarding his son, who as to his human nature was a descendant of David, and who through the spirit of holiness was declared with the power to be the Son of God by his resurrection from the dead: Jesus Christ our Lord.

Through him and for his name's sake, we received grace and apostleship to call people from among all the Gentiles to the obedience that comes from faith.

And you, also, are among those who are called to

belong to Jesus Christ.
  Grace to you from God our Father and from the Lord Jesus Christ . . . and . . . peace.

ABOUT THE AUTHOR

Dan Neidermyer is a widely-known playwright, novelist, and producer-director of live theatre, video, and film productions.

Originally from Ephrata, Pennsylvania, he founded several theatre and video production companies following his graduation from Philadelphia College of Bible and post-graduate work at Temple University, Reformed Episcopal Seminary, and Millersville University.

He established Maranatha Productions, Inc., a non-profit production company, to communicate biblical truths, principles, and insights with the use of drama. As executive producer and director, he has developed several drama teams that have performed throughout the United States, Canada, the West Indies, and Europe at churches, camps, youth rallies, prisons, convalescent homes, nursing homes, and hospitals.

During a twelve-year stint as Associate Lecturer of Communications at the Evangelical School of Theology in Myerstown, Pennsylvania, playwright-director Neidermyer taught seminarians and educators how to develop and use drama, radio, and television to share biblical messages.

He has also taught seminarians in Sweden where he returns yearly to teach and develop a drama team that travels throughout Scandinavia and the United States. He also teaches in Jamaica. His biblical dramatizations have been translated into several languages including Swedish and Patwa, a Jamaican folk dialect, for production within the West Indies.

Dan Neidermyer's home is in Columbus, Ohio. He spends much time also in Dixon, Illinois where he maintains offices for live theatre production. His video production work, however, is done primarily in Columbus.

ORDER FORM

MERIWETHER PUBLISHING LTD.
P.O. BOX 7710
COLORADO SPRINGS, CO 80933
TELEPHONE: (303)594-4422

Please send me the following books:

_____**Scripture Plays** $9.95
by Dan Neidermyer #PP-B150
A book of plays dramatizing the Holy Bible

_____**Costuming the Christmas and Easter Play** $5.95
by Alice M. Staeheli #PP-B180
How to costume any religious play

_____**The Complete Banner Handbook** $10.95
by Janet Litherland #PP-B172
A complete guide to banner design and construction

_____**The Official Sunday School Teachers** $7.95
Handbook
by Joanne Owens #PP-B152
*An indispensable aid and barrel of laughs for anyone
involved in Sunday school activities*

_____**The Clown Ministry Handbook** $7.95
by Janet Litherland #PP-B163
The first and most complete text on the art of clown ministry

_____**Fundraising for Youth** $8.95
by Dorthy M. Ross #PP-B184
*Hundreds of wonderful ways of raising funds for youth
organizations*

_____**Getting Started in Drama Ministry** $8.95
by Janet Litherland #PP-B154
A complete guide to Christian drama

> *I understand that I may return any book
> for a full refund if not satisfied.*

NAME: _____

ORGANIZATION NAME: _____

ADDRESS: _____

CITY: _____STATE: _____ZIP: _____

PHONE: _____

☐ **Check Enclosed**
☐ **Visa or Master Card #**_____

Signature: _____
(required for Visa/Mastercard orders)

COLORADO RESIDENTS: Please add 3% sales tax.
SHIPPING: Include $1.50 for the first book and 50¢ for each additional
book ordered.

☐ *Please send me a copy of your complete catalog of books or plays.*